BETWEEN WORDS AND SILENCE

BETWEEN

Words and Silence

Zsuzsa Beney

Translated by Mark Griffith

Mare's Nest

Published in 1999
by Mare's Nest Publishing
41 Addison Gardens London W14 0DP

Between Words and Silence
Zsuzsa Beney

Copyright © Zsuzsa Beney 1993
Translation copyright © Mark Griffith 1999
Introduction copyright © George Szirtes 1999

Cover photograph and design Squid Inc.
Typeset by Agnesi Text Hadleigh Suffolk
Printed and bound by Antony Rowe Chippenham Wiltshire

ISBN 1 899197 50 8

Szó És Csend Között was originally published by Könyvek Budapest 1993.

This book is published with the financial assistance of the Arts Council of England.

CONTENTS

INTRODUCTION

George Szirtes

'For now we see through a glass, darkly,' says St Paul in his First Epistle to the Corinthians; 'but then', he continues, 'face to face.' That, in essence, has been the theme of all mystical writing. 'Short prayer pierceth heaven,'[1] said the anonymous medieval author of *The Cloud of Unknowing* echoing St Augustine, encouraging us to 'smite that thick cloud of unknowing with a sharp dart of longing love'. Once smitten, the cloud might reveal the true rapture in things. The fourteenth-century German mystic Suso exhorts his young follower Elizabeth Stäglin to 'Look upwards, then, with sparkling eyes and radiant face and bounding heart, and behold Him . . . See how, by gazing on this mirror, there springs up speedily, in a soul susceptible of such impression, an intense inward jubilee.'[2]

But jubilee, rapture, ecstasy, visions and miracles exist only in the wilder outbacks of our period. For us, says Rilke in his First Duino Elegy, there remains

> some tree on a slope, to be looked at day after day,
> there remains for us yesterday's walk and the long drawn loyalty
> of a habit that liked us and stayed and never gave notice.[3]

Though, to continue with a different translation, that is not all, for there remains night,

> when a wind full of infinite space
> gnaws at our faces . . .[4]

The notion of the transcendental does not leave us: the passion for it remains, fed by love, desire, loss, pain, humiliation, despair and the approach of death. In such circumstances we feel the world echo with our predicament. We apprehend how our apprehension of it throughout has been tangential, symbolic, interpretive, transformational; that our internal and external realities are, and always have been, so closely identified it would be hard, indeed probably beyond us, to draw the precise line between them. The night continues gnawing at our faces even when the angels we perceive are terrible rather than consoling, and that the tree on the slope, for all the fact that we are habituated to it, is a hybrid and an enigma. As Rilke (Mitchell's translation) says:

. . . the living are wrong to believe
in the too-sharp distinctions which they themselves have created.

The essays of the Hungarian poet Zsuzsa Beney are explorations of the areas where these 'too-sharp distinctions' no longer obtain. They first appeared in Hungarian in 1993, in the author's sixty-third year, in that period which, for an individual, is neither quite middle age, nor yet precisely old age; and in a transitional historical epoch which, for her country, was no longer represented by the old regime but in which the new order had not (nor has it yet, we should add) established itself.

This 'in-betweenness' is abhorred by politicians of all colours in all countries because it refuses rhetoric, sloganization, sound-bites and head-lines. The Hungary of the old regime was a superstructure of shadows – shadow economies, shadow categories, shadow responsibilities, shadow power – built on a rhetorical foundation of clarities: Party–Non Party, Communism–Capitalism, employment–unemployment, war–peace, East–West. The greatest poets of the major post-war period were all, to some degree, explorers of the shadow, seeking the mystical in the mundane: Weöres with his cosmologies, Pilinszky with his horrors and calvaries; Nemes Nagy with her crystalline geologies and topographies; all reject the world of the public pragmatic lie and strive for some under-standing of the private, possibly universal, truth. In her sensibility, instincts and terms of reference, Beney belongs with them.

These essays are then not so much essays as poems, or at least poetic explorations of metaphysical subjects. They come to us without scholarly apparatus, without a fixed framework of philosophical categories, with-out any pretence of establishing an objective state of affairs. What they attempt to articulate are intuitions about a sense of shifting reality. They move about inside the cloud of unknowing with a vague sense that there may be some radiance available beyond them, but with the clear con-sciousness of the responsibility of describing those clouds as accurately as possible. These clouds constitute a form of reality in themselves, and in so far as they do so they have an objective existence which may be mapped through memory, metaphor, fear and desire, in terms that do not themselves prove wholly cloudy and evanescent.

The glass through which we see darkly is first represented by the surface of a lake that reflects the sky. At twilight 'the things of the world turn black . . . the treetops become the dark spires of an illusory city'. This is read as an omen but it 'can promise no path to redemption'. Nevertheless the sense of seeing something that can be interpreted as an omen persists. 'It is', she says, 'as if at the very surface, at the pane of impermeable glass, they [those shifting patterns of colour, the human hand with its fingers, lost souls] should suddenly unite with their other selves, their heavenly spirits, their true selves.'

This may at first appear to be a complex baggage, almost too heavily laden with associations and assumptions: those lost souls moving among the spires of a gothic city are freighted with literary and psychological history. Time and again, Beney recognizes this, perceives it as a kind of Maya or illusion and moves on, only to face it in some other form. It is desire and loss that drive her on to seek 'a unity with the Beloved'. We sense the natural mirror of the lake's surface 'so much as a boundary that we perceive his gaze sunken into the bottomless depths of passion'. This, for her, is a cause of personal agony as the Beloved – Him I loved – has vanished.

In this respect the essays may be read as a kind of lament for someone loved and lost. The exploration then is of grief and the sense of prolonged presence.

The first metaphor is the lake, the second the twilight between dawn and morning. To walk out at this time is to wander through 'a maze' in 'the cities of our memories and desires' where 'the city squares melt into each other'. It is, like James (B.V.) Thomson's *City of Dreadful Night*, full of cobwebs and lagoons. As Beney says, 'it interdicts our experiencing the actuality of the world', and at this point she presents us with an extraordinary vision of cherubim who are 'looking outward, north, south, east and west, yet gazing directly into each other's eyes, even when they stand back to back'.

These are visions and symbols and are probably most usefully amenable to discussion in terms of poetics. Here we can see how the mundane presents us with layers of literary association: a garden seen through a kitchen window brings to mind certain cold mornings before the speaker and the beloved first met, which recalls the actual meetings remembered as 'brilliant explosions' and pentecostal 'tongues of flame'. After this initial burst of establishing imagery we return to the garden and the trees and the air itself, which contain a series of states of mind, such as love, apprehension, despair and thoughts of death presented as metaphors: tapestries, games, crowns and fabrics. So later, childhood is conjured in terms of grapes, apples, rooms and clouds; desire is associated with mud and rodents and death with mildew and more mud. Out of all this the poet builds a mystic tower of lamentation, whose bricks are those emblematic memories and experiences of the mundane world and whose mortar is the compound of emotions through which these emblematic memories are brought to consciousness. The tower rises through the energy provided by desire and grief, and through an apprehension of the potential radiance beyond the clouds that are the towers' natural environment. Earth with its trees, grapes, rooms and rodents below for foundation; the metaphors of tapestries, games, crowns, mazes and spires laid over that to buttress the building at the level of the imagination, and then, beyond that, the mystical drive to ascend through the painful abstractions of love, loss, etc. It is not only the *Duino Elegies* but *The Four Quartets* that come to mind here.

Before the pragmatists, empiricists and rationalist withdraw from all this cloudiness into their sensibly lit enclaves, they should remember that human experience not only includes the realms of longing and longing, in particular, for transcendence, but that this longing has an ancient history of generative power. The lakes we walk by do seem to contain intimations of worlds beyond the immediately sensible one, and the apprehension of these worlds generates creative energies by which the most rational of us are not only consoled but energized into feeling and thought.

1   *The Cloud of Unknowing*, edited by Evelyn Underhill (1912).
2   Suso, quoted in Evelyn Underhill, *The Mystics of the Church* (1964).
3   Rainer Maria Rilke, First Duino Elegy, from *Duino Elegies*, translated by Leishman and Spender (1975).
4   Rainer Maria Rilke, First Duino Elegy, from *The Selected Poetry of Rainer Maria Rilke*, translated by Stephen Mitchell (1987).

BETWEEN
Poetry and Prose

Let us consider the existence of God. Such existence cannot be proved by evidence but only by faith. In a curious way this not-provable proof, this inadmissible evidence, almost breaks through the unfaith of my own being. Such existence – indescribable in terms of existence itself – becomes poignantly actual when mirrored in the actuality of the world.

As if parallel to these mirrored elements, language sets its demonic traps within us, summoning, seemingly only by the optical illusions of light and shade, transparency and opacity, a miasma of forms, governed solely by our changing perspective into the depths. Within and without us, an infinite number of possible variations co-exist in the vibrant and incomprehensible instantaneous present. Because of the momentary grace afforded me to gaze into the depths of realness, it is possible for me from time to time to substitute for this word 'realness' the word 'reality'.

Here is the proof I am moving towards with such care and qualification: our existence embraces a view of a lake, the perception of which image we could not grasp were it not for the refracted rays of light gathered together within our eyes. At some profound level we understand that no other image could be the same without containing this same sky and this same mirroring of sky, or containing this same sense of height and depth, the which cannot itself be held up for inspection by the tweezers of reality or of illusion, nor by the tweezers of realness or presentiment, nor of prescience (metaphor of grace) nor, to speak once more of illusion (the essence of emotion being deceit of the senses), nor can it be held by the tweezers of existence or of non-existence.

A mysterious vision offers itself to us on the surface of the lake. It is that uncertain twilight hour when the things of the world turn black – as the sky as yet does not – when the treetops become the dark spires of an illusory city, or appear as if in some distant landscape, as in the demi-history evoked by old photographs and paintings, metamorphosed by desire and memory. In this distant landscape the turrets of the cypress trees in this garden at dusk stand against a sky from which all colour has been drained away, sucked out. At this moment it is neither un-blue, nor un-grey, yet still not become black and thus its absolute lack of colour inspires thoughts of nothingness of the void. Mirrored on the onyx black of the surface of the lake, the trees are present in yet another shade of black – trees that but a half-hour since were rich in the deep reds, browns, purples of the light of the sun. This is a mystery – seen by us alone as a mystery, or rather within the world itself as an omen – that reveals itself in the simultaneous height and depth of the lake, reminding us of the essential shallowness of the lake. Yet how may this essential shallowness assume the height of the sky itself, which reverted in depth no plumbline might fathom?

But the tree, its bark marble white, bone white, yellow white, invites the palms of our hands with its marble smoothness, promising pleasure beyond sensuousness, and stirring aesthetic emotions appropriate to the appreciation of art. The great trunk of the tree divides at a man's height, reminding us of psychological projection: two bodies but a single soul; two lovers but a single body. On the surface of the water the tree in reflection takes on a lewd identity: the smoothness of a perverse naked-ness, at the splitting of the trunk, at the point of division, a tuft of grass, arousing not the excitement of teasing, chaste concealment, but the dubious shudder of ambigious hermaphroditism. The downward spreading of its branches – or are they roots? – intensifies further our awareness of its physicality. This bi-directionally growing, leaf-shedding tree demonstrates that this mirror surface is bordered simultaneously by sky and by marshland. This mirror surface inhabits the human soul, stretching into infinity, and, like pools of water in the twilight of our dreams, this smooth, hard, glass pane can promise no path to redemp-tion. Even should it crack, it cannot separate and create an opening within itself.

And yet . . . in the gentle autumn sunshine the fluttering of a veil demarcates the rigidity of the mirror and the burgeoning of Protean nature. From the depths – ever darker than the heights – rush-purple leaves begin to float upwards, drifting towards the surface. From beneath the invisible takes form, slowly rising, just as in the old pictures redeemed souls ascended to the heights of heaven. Leaves move from the sky below towards a sky above, from some hellish parody of the vaulted heavens to the breezy heights, passing through the solidity, the rigidity and the mirroring glass up in to the airiness of the sky, where we may sense insubstantial, translucent currents gently flowing.

All this leads us towards a belief in miracle and ascension. These shifting patterns of colour, so fine they seem almost two-dimensional, seem like the leaves of a tree; they also remind us of the human hand – the human hand with fingers extended, seeking, feeling, touching, caressing. And – and this is almost beyond words – they are reminiscent of lost souls wandering within the depths-become-heights, fleeing not only our world where the senses are deceived, but from human existence *because* the senses are deceived, and reaching upward, soaring now, winging freely away. It is as if at the very surface, at the pane of impermeable glass, they should suddenly unite with their other selves, their heavenly spirits, their true selves, undeceivable, desired, created and marked with the glittering trace of the hand of God. Then, in that very moment, tantalizingly, they would disappear and become as nothing.

I come here each dawn and each dusk, not only to gaze on the lake and the plane tree, bone smooth, at the water's edge, but also to look into the ever-dark mirror, where the taut, rigid water, as sensitive and precise as a column of mercury in some scientific instrument, bears witness to the formation of mist as the invisible is chilled into visibility, to the increasing density of the air as the growing warmth of the sun condenses the moisture within it. The cold, metallic smells of leaf mould provoke memory fragments, like floating islands, bearing the childhood scent of grapes and apples, and bringing me poetry. I come here each dawn and each dusk, not only to gaze on the lake and the plane tree, bone smooth at the water's edge, to hear in my daydreams the ticking of time itself, but also to partake in the decay of heavenly purity as it descends into the underworld, until the surface of the lake is obscured by a fishing-net blanket of damp, tattered rushes and the dark green tangle of frogspawn. I come here, rather, to observe the eternal transposition of time and timelessness, the constant confluence of free-flowing rivers, for the ancient path defined again and again by familiar steps and for the unimaginable image of words forming, frosted, in the air. I continue on my way, walking more slowly than I would wish, in order to continue the fragmentary dialogue in place of which I might once have wished for dreaming isolation. And it is here that again and again, as if I were inserting beneath my fingernails thorns from the stinging branches of the wild lemon tree, I acknowledge the unbearable pain of a world in which it is possible to address the One who does not exist.

Yes, the world is unbearable. Existence is reflected back on itself in the shivering breeze of time – time that can, in a single day, sweep into nothingness the immense, near-spherical crown of this oak tree, this flame-red vision, this world tree, and yet is capable not only of maintaining it within our disintegrating memory, but also in its *Doppelgänger*, trapped between mirrors where that which once existed can never transmute into any other state. There is a distinction between the non-existence of having died and the non-existence of never having been born. Our disintegrating memory fixes the transient image for all eternity into the nothingness of that which once existed and does so no longer. It recalls the phenomenon of the autumn tree constructed of immeasurably large and immeasurably small units of time. It is concrete: it is not an image; it is not a flame; it is not even a cosmic emblem – not even when unobserved by human eye. Forked lightning divides in two the intertwined unison of the yet-to-be-seen scarlet crown and the seen scarlet crown and penetrates deep into the heart and from the wound it makes, deeper than the heart's depth, love spurts like a spring. It is love for Him who floats in death both in the memory's transience, hovering above the surface of the lake and in the actual, never-vanishing non-existence of the water's depths.

The surface of the lake is unimaginably hard. I am tempted to describe it as being like bark, but this would imply the ingrained trunks of trees, brown, uncurling layers, and evoke in our sense of touch the feel of the roughest of substances. But, on the contrary, what I am describing, the surface itself, is one of the most tangible insubstantial elements in our world. The boundary, the surface itself, is not itself water, although from below there is a film of water, as fine as a hair's breadth; and neither is it air, although from above there is the finest veil of air. The insubstantial boundary between water and air – a mathematical point describing the evaporating planes defined by the ripplings and tortions of the skirts of the dry land – doubly reminds us of the sense of a particular substance, as if when we look *into* it we are also looking *at* it, and simultaneously we perceive the water as both a vast mass of glass and as the external reality reflected on its surface. On its underside is creation's mysterious silver coating. Thus does the secret mystery within this familiar landscape invite us to imagine the transition – itself beyond comprehension – between the two impermeable surfaces. This is a transition that renders impossible our falling in love with that One with whom we are already acquainted in the superior surface of this worldly space should He step for all eternity below into the dark depths of a water that has ceased to reflect reality. Yet we should be granted the possibility of falling in love with one of these eternally submerged bodiless imaginings – drowned as we may be in the higher agonies of physical existence.

But is it even possible for us to achieve a unity with the Beloved – with the Beloved's face, looking out at us as if from the laminated surface of an old photograph, a picture of an insubstantial imagining and the elements contained within the picture, which is itself no less than the reality of existence we call life? The answer is the natural mirror of the lake's surface. We sense this so much as a boundary that we perceive his gaze sunken into the bottomless depths of passion. From the depths in surfaces into the baroque vortices of the swirling clouds, until it is almost lost in Godly suffering in the heights – the suffering of God the creator who alone knows the depths of the ever-turbulent maeström fomenting in the well-shaft of hell. This gaze alone rendered for me the earthly world describable and bodily pain as proof of a further indescribable, inexplicable agony – an agony infinitely profound, a world-birthing agony. I needed to see this face and these eyes closed and covered with gauze, because I needed to gaze in the dark, laminated surface of the lake in order for grace to be granted me, for my suffering to dissolve along with its duplication in the mystery of the mirror image that does not reflect my very self. And finally will the question – might we – or I – find unity with Him whom we loved – Him whom I loved – will the question appear to us – or to me – utterly without meaning?

BETWEEN

Dawn and Morning

This is the time, as the hands of the clock nudge past each other through the low-numbered hours, audible only as the muted click of a marked minute, as the darkness and dawn inter-dissolve, that we pass, our senses alive, from the ice-cold, star-studded night into the stone-hard, ice-cruel day. Not through the gap between dawn and morning, its walls crumbling. In reality – but how real is reality, given the ready deceit of our senses? – with this slow stirring within a frighteningly strange town, more alien than any other alien place, we must accept we have already crossed the divide between night and dawn, and we are entering a further bleak depth.

We walk into this depth, the surface of the walls obscured by thick fog, encrusted eternally by ice, snow, hoarfrost, frozen into stalagtites. All we hold to be the essence of our humanity, our senses, our imagination, stands perpendicular to our route downward, downward into this crevice at our feet. As the frost crackles at our step, we know our way, but a way that lies in twin directions, the path that guides our footfalls and yet within us, beneath us, twisting and turning, another path and, as we tread its frozen sands, we pass over it in another direction. This moment, as we walk, exists between night and dawn, and yet another moment, separate from us, marks our transition from dawn to morning, in a virtual space that translates the unimaginability of time itself within our consciousness into another language, a language we recognize and yet whose syntax we cannot understand. So as we walk on, the hoarfrost crackling beneath our feet, the concrete ringing at our step, we touch the iron chain heavy with ice; step by step we sense the blackness of the night, the unconscious world of dream, slowly giving way to that deeper unconsciousness – hopelessness – and sleep's solitude pressing the soul between leaden plates of despair. Sleep's solitude presses on the soul, which – its reality unreal – was ripped out of time the moment it was ripped from its companion – that companion who, with the glittering light of his love, drew the dawn from the night and drew the morning from the dawn – mornings that in summer are first hazy and then a golden green and that in winter are blacker than blackness itself. When will his absence enable me to follow in the footsteps of Orpheus, to take that step, to turn and pursue that lost vision, to take a step beyond the final tread of the stairway and let myself fall, fall into the spiralling vortex of time as, simultaneously, I am both pulled towards him and driven infinitely far away from him?

But, if we are lost, if we are become as nothing, if we are dissolved into a timeless time, into this transmutating softness between night and dawn, between dawn and morning, what hardness would have been formed within the human heart, what kind of God could have set it there to mark the passing time like the arm of a sun-dial, the arm of a moon-dial – indicating time passing with twilight's shadow transcending the darkness, marking passing time, making time measurable – which we understand as the supreme mystery of our existence – measurable simply with numbers. Numbers mean so much more than words and yet are so much more difficult to understand. Because of this, their exactitude allows us to experience the eternally inexact (the superficiality of which may indeed be the essential mirrored as the superficial). These numbers approach more nearly the distinction between time passing within us and time passing in the world around us. We are aware of the mysterious river of time, flowing, foaming and tumbling beneath the surface crust, the eternal eddying and metamorphosing of space. Were we then to become as nothing, ourselves absorbed into this eternal transformation, how could we imagine we could re-orient ourselves any better in terms of space than we could in terms of time? Were we to lose ourselves in the spiralling vortices transforming night to dawn, dawn to morning, how could we but lose our way in this maze, whose walls express the darkness of this unknown city and whose streets echo with our dreams of cities at night? These are the cities of our memories and desires, cities we have walked through, cities whose squares and streets are the products of desire and expectation, in which alleyways lead to the crown of a ridge and a turned corner reveals an unknown vista; these are cities more real than this one, now left behind as a car glides through in the darkness. There are colours living in the depths of the darkness. It is as if in the gloomy twilight we recognize the familiar labyrinthine and receding soul of the object of our desire. Now this soul, emerging from dream, desire, the ancient deep places of this world or not quite of this world, appears simultaneously both firmly familiar and yet unknown, frozen in the eternal darkness – just as in this winter dawn the city squares melt into each other, overlapping, masking each other, revealing their ancient depths to a faculty of sight deeper than that of the physical eye. This is a reality beyond words, beyond touch, within the grasp only of dream, a country it is possible to map only by the glowing embers of the dark. I do not know if this landscape is the mysterious country of love. If so, then it is true that lovers wander within each others' souls. They wander through this city, known equally profoundly to them both, yet with neither having ever seen, either singly or together, the cobweb of its streets and lagoons.

Time engraves its image the one upon the other, an endless merging of endlessly merging vistas, the fluid intermingling of layer and layer, and, thus, the unbroken re-forming of instantaneous eternity. This interdicts our experiencing time continuous and time passing. The mingling of this place with the places within our memories – so like and so unlike what we have remarked upon before – interdicts our experiencing the actuality of the world. This double interdiction, without limit and without definition, itself removes the world from our experience, the world that is real only and alone in the rays of light mirrored into the eyes of the beloved other, the lines of light between eye and eye, the warp and weft of a complex cloth. One fibre torn and the unity of the world unravels – a unity that is perhaps without existence because it is without the dimension of space. The living wound bleeds a healing tissue of fibres, a cobweb for our consciousness. Thus we cannot perceive whether it is space that brings healing or the disease itself, the disease of the sick soul. The same holds good for the concept of 'the world', for which could be substituted the concept of 'space'. That which we perceive and experience as space, and into the open area of which we wander with such dread, we perceive as the narrow corridors of a maze, the labyrinth ever being the symbolic home of the other, either human or non-human. We see the faces of cherubim, looking outward, north, south, east and west, yet gazing directly into each others' eyes, even when they stand back to back. They gaze out in opposite directions, yet all gaze directly towards each other. Their looping, straight gazes enmesh all existence into a globe-shaped lattice and all that holds it together are the ungraspable and insubstantial lines of their gazing, about which we can know nothing beyond the source and the conclusion. This gazing is as concrete as the path between gate and gate; it perceives and yet is itself imperceptible; it absorbs and perhaps radiates colour, yet is itself colourless; it has form within the dimension of space and yet is itself unmeasurable in terms of space, weaving a mesh from its own dimensionless and insubstantial translucency. If the dimensions of space and time own so much reality that reality may not be expressed by one single truth, and, therefore, existence does not take form from this reality, then how may we understand the wonderful revelation of this gaze melting into our own gaze, melting also into the revelation of God as gaze; how may we understand the reality of those angelic faces and that our own gaze, taken up by other eyes, may not even ensure the non-reality of our imagination, the eternal insubstantiality of reality?

This absolute point on the earth is my home for this sequence of days. It could never be my true home (because I have foregone my right and my opportunity ever to experience this world as my home), but for fragmentary moments in the continuum of time it was my home, from this very point, out of this very soil of hopelessness that I had to rip myself, uproot myself, as if I grew in that soil like a tree. Yes, uproot myself and fly like a bird, darting through the leaves on the branches of a tree in the summer dusk, seen only after it has vanished, the bird itself present only for the twinkling of an eye, the disturbed foliage the only indication of its existence, the rustle of the leaves like the whisper of wings. Why here, for one single unbearable moment in the light of the setting sun, that I must become a bird, my wing feathers bright in the red light that still blooms in the milk-like mist, the light that seems to have no source as we sense the sun has already, for all eternity, sunk below the horizon. Perhaps the beating of a wing, at a precise angle, would coax light once more from the underworld, light that knows no time, that knows no end, knows nothing beyond its own ecstasy, in which ecstasy it may not know whether it perceives its own bright illumination or the flash of a bird's feather in flight, or its own bright illumination reflected in the beating of a wing, which has become, at this nebulous indeterminate dream level of idea and memory, at once blue and green, the wing of a roller-bird, of a bee-eater, of a woodpecker, at once red and green. Or yet a feather from the wing of an ice-bird, of Alcestis, hovering above a lost life, a lover abandoned to the currents of the air, zigzagging ever closer, drawn by the power of an unknown lure. In one absolute moment it reaches the eternally beloved, brushing his shoulder and stirring the silky fine flowing locks, and in the scent of that hair moving in the air, recognizes him who had long since forgotten the sinister, dark, utterly solemn feast. Long since he had forgotten the girl setting out on her journey with a serious look in her eyes: a farewell but not a parting.

She set out as if approaching death and the burden of the fear of death weighed on her shoulders like lead. The girl, in reality, disappeared and now, formless, bodyless, memory rises and falls with the currents of air carrying this evocative scent, the nearness of a human body. Why did I, my roots grasping deep into this acid clay, in the physical death agony of my hopelessness, allow this bird to fly free, to rise again and again with the hopeful and hopeless currents of air, in its unrupturable eternal dance, whose end is an endless dance of death? In the glowing embers of the setting sun should I, as if myself flying, engage with the suffering that transcends hopelessness, with the light that transcends darkness? Should I perceive the eternal fires of the setting sun as a boundary between dawn and morning, flowing from a darker darkness into a deeper dark, as evening thickens into the utter darkness of night?

The shading of evening into night is the shading of sleep into death is the shading of autumn – helplessly and driven by the movement of time, moving by its inner laws in observation of the majesty of nature – into winter. Duty and awe fill the human heart, and resignation – near-acceptance – too, because the thickening of the darkness does not imply the ending of existence but rather a sinking into the darkness of God's deeper, softer darkness: liquid, as it were; underground, as it were; gaseous currents, as it were. We are speaking here of sinking, not of falling; of returning, not of leaving. But when, this December night, dawn becomes morning, it becomes a morning that is daytime without daylight, and when that daylight arrives, it will not bring with it translucence and the determinate brightness of colour, but a monochrome greyness, mingling browns and greys, merging into a boundless dusk that stifles and contains colour. For that very reason the sunlight cannot burn through the dense cloud cover. In this shrouded landscape light distinguishes slowly between the shiny and the matt, between black and the fog formed of browns and greys and the unnameable yellow of a world on the edge of death. We perceive a process whereby the blackness that engulfed everything now begins itself slowly to dissolve: after the first intense difficulty of the spasm that causes a distinguishable fragment to break free of the indefinable mass, the process loosens and shakes the world that was until this point capable only of grasping its identity as a dense totality. But the nature of its density was the density of the void in a sanctified vessel, attending and accepting all that flows into it until at capacity it bursts, the void itself demands to be filled. But this morning is not a demonstration of the process whereby the first molecule separates from the unmeasurable mass, whereby black dilutes towards white, whereby the closed approaches the open, whereby the determination of God becomes the freedom of God, and this relaxation can permit the emergence of colour from the depths of matter, can grant space to air, can rekindle the inner flame from the exhausted embers – that inner flame that brings wonder and understanding to our eyes: the red, the green, the blue, the violet. No, this is a morning when, after the cold of the night and the dawn, molecules still adhere to each other, and when, although there might be space to stir, the soil, the grass, the maize stalks, the bare frosted branches, all dissolves not into colours but into tones. This lies heavy on our souls, as it lies heavy on the flight of birds in this narrow band between sky and ground, compressing the flowering circles of the night into hopelessness, a density forbidding expansion, driving the temperature lower, degrading the world into a colourless mass.

These are mornings for journeys, for arrivals and departures, half in the day and yet still in the night, in the daylight of the soul, as we become a part of the truth of the world, and in the night of the soul, to be precise in the first moments of the breaking of the day, on the verge of wakefulness, as we roam the world of our dreams, where the cities are built of a different brick than the cities of the day, in which we wander down a different kind of alleyway, past different churchspires and different parks, where there is a lake with swans and where beyond the city limits there are miles and miles of rubbish dumps, all different from those of the cities of the day: these cities, like the figures on a deck of playing cards, are mirror images of the cities of the day. We cannot tell which is the mirror image. Have we been taught to see by our dreams, or do we dream that there was once something we saw and then forgot, or that once we imagined the visions and fairy-tales of our desires? Narrative and memory and desire, more profound than the sketches or the fragments of film from the beginning of our century, all conjure this morning's railway station. It is a great high building, beside which crouch the dwarfed houses. There are buildings inside this building, constructed to another scale, within an open square which is also an enclosed area; there are small pavilions and the painted ceiling in the style of some decorated Renaissance palace, but it is done in such a way that we recognize the style of the imitating hand that created it, and the stamp of the taste of the period that guided that imitating hand. We can see high above the scaffolding, built to reinforce and reconstruct the endlessly redrawn outlines of this fantastic circus erected on this enormous fairground, the huge plaster figures of the merry-go-rounds emblematic of our childlike wonder. Beside the scaffolding lie the discarded elements: the vast clock and the air itself, redefined into blocks by the fissures. This entire vision gives a frame and definition to the fluttering within as all that passes here below is experienced as if frozen in time. The teeming of an anthill is to our eyes a rippling permanence, heaving and re-forming in its prescribed motionlessness like some static mound. From this emerge twitching black specks in straight lines and meandering lines. We need to bend close to the earth and sand of the summer meadow to discern the ebb and flow of the patterning movement. And here, in the underwater halls, clambering out of nooks and crannies, like beetles from their night-time refuges, in filthy rags, stinking of cheap booze and fags, swearing out of their despair and wretchedness, clinging together, their faces grimed with pain, suffering so much more than we ourselves, emerge all the promises and guarantees of our redemption. This picture fills our field of vision like some tangible fabric and provides a background for the surprising and astounding flight of the pigeons between the scaffolding and the ceiling as they fly up from the casing of the vast clock and then return, having penetrated the outer darkness. The actuality of these birds tears away the illusion of the reality of their souls and also of this body, which, at this precise moment, here in the waiting room of a southern Hungarian railway station, senses around itself the hall into which it hurried, without a glance at the platforms, lugging the leaden weight of this leaden farewell. This extraordinary vision – the painted walls, the scaffolding, the miserable wretches and the pigeons, those grotesque parodies of the Paraclete – ensures solely that this as yet undreamt of hell shall yawn for all eternity.

Is it conceivable that these pigeons, with their surprising and astounding appearance, bring a sense of the non-reality of existence – which is generally perceived by us as the existence of a devilish reality, smelling of the earth, smelling of the winter, a gruesome, endless certainty, the essence of which is a sense of a defeated non-certainty, the realization of the deception of our senses permeating our entire being and yet this realization itself never achieving the threshold of our thoughts – existence which is for us solely a function of imitation. It is always the case that we perceive the existence of illusion as more actual than those phenomena that surround us and seem real to others. This very morning, in this very place, in the wild and misty cold, the iron chain is frozen, its clinking mute, a chill rises from the soil, our toes in our boots are stiff with cold, as are our fingers in their skin-like fine leather gloves. The morning lamplight does not illumine with a bright clear light but with a murky yellow the stone bench smeared with mud, scattered papers, cigarette ends, blood, mucus and other excretions of the human body. This journey between dawn and morning, flaking away the scales of night from the actuality of the body, moves between dream and wakefulness, where the image radiating towards the outer world from within is subject to the compressing force of the crystallizing air from without, causing the sense of physical reality to shimmer and vacillate. It would seem that the non-real body would perceive this vision as actuality – which takes on the quality of illusion only because it is so unexpected – the pigeons flying within the hall walls, their circling surprising and astounding, different from any other movement in this world, for within the realization of the deception of our senses we cannot conceive of the possibility of their flight in and out of the yawning fissures high in the walls beyond the reach of our sight. These winged souls appear and disappear in the medium we can name only as cold, only as darkness. At this time, in this place, these words cannot define the dual lifeforms that are the qualities – not the essence – of matter, which with our old words we defined as inifinite density. This vision now appears to our trembling senses as a perversion of itself, non-real, non-actual. And thus, matter that does not exist, robbed of the reality of its physical existence by that same sudden transsubstantiation as that involved in the intensity of the perception of reality disguised by the illusion of the actual, may be perceived only as a function of the material. And thus, in this place, in this non-existant aperture between dawn and morning, there seems to open up an existant aperture, a rupture in time, where a falling, a divorce from the laws of gravity, a meandering with the air, takes form and colour, and with plaster, paint, scaffolding and lamplight creates from its very self the walls of this hall. Thus we metamorphose into the birds that inhabit the abyss between the earth and the air. We become the illusion that is these birds, and the creators of this illusion too, none other than a fanciful circling from dark to light and from light to dark, bearing on our feathers drops of dawn dew, melting and remelting again and again in this murky light. The concourse of that particular station is so very far away and so very long ago but in an unseen dawn, perhaps the pigeons never fly, these non-existing yet apparent birds which are but a trace of a fleeting memory, flocking at the edges of the hall, which is itself in the process of transsubstantiation between the timefulness of the past and the timelessness of never. These birds of death, which not for ever yet continually renew the realization of the deception of our senses of our separation, a separation I identify on this occasion with mute and bloodless death, again and again rekindle a flame with the beating of their wings from the dull glowing red embers of madness.

This is the selfsame flame that snuffs out the oily blackness of dawn and leaves in its place the morning soot, an iron-grey soot that lies thick on the twin rails, on the buildings, on everything alongside the railway cuttings throughout half the country, on everything alongside the railway track for mile after mile, hour after hour, as from an immeasurable distance into an immeasurable time the train journeys with us. There is the sky, sinking from its zenith to its nadir, even when forgotten unforgettable, and what we might in our trembling name 'Evil' as it oozes eternally from under the railway sleepers like marsh water out of the sodden earth, the exaltation and the helplessnes, the ecstasy and the sense of abandonment, the forked pliers grasping the stalk until we are no longer able to ascertain what is up and what is down, and whether it is space or time swirling around us. We cannot know whether our hope like an ocean wave surges above the surf of our hopelessness, or breaks back into its own foam, unable to distinguish the differing deadly passions of abandonment. As long as this unknown and awesome power voids our belief in what our senses tell us of the reality of the world, within us or without us, transforming into its own mirrored reality, the morning colours the hoarfrost virginal white in the depth of night becoming murky in the actuality of its own light. The frozen lace on the trees and bushes appears solid, material, and yet is in reality liquid. It gives definition to the branches and colours their nakedness, almost matching the tints of the earth, which will soon be a nothingness. We can scarcely understand this, how what once had form, was crystalline, bark containing nothing, might soon disappear, be gone utterly and for ever, with no memory left behind. What memory survives will be but the illusion of this morning, a memory of a memory, a picture without actuality, a picture of a picture of the future of an unperceivable memory, which through the multiplying links of this chain is connected more directly to something that we now perceive as reality, as what might be better described as 'the present'. More directly connected than the buds to the branches of the trees, more directly than the fruit that will at some later date emerge from these buds, which took their shape almost randomly and accidentally, like some sketch drawn by the light and limp creepers of this hoarfrost. No, not accidentally, because these are not simply silvered drawings of the future, because we perceive in them the first unravelling of apple blossom a million million years since, as indivisible from petals, snow, crystals, held deep in time as indivisible from the reality of this heart-breaking sight, from the slanting sunbeams of dusk or dawn, the knowledge of the final reality of a passing moment that will be followed so often by the knowledge of the final reality. This is no mistake, for all moments are final moments as it is given to us to live the moment that is not final as if it were final, and to continue to preserve it as if it were indeed final, again melting and remelting the ever-numbing ice. We desire that the fact of our passing may not be a dreadful molecular stasis, nor the silence of frosted windows expanding eternally into eternal space, and in the cold not the twanging of snapped twigs, but a continuing pain, opening like the fissure between night and dawn, between dawn and morning, a well drawn from darkness deep into darkness, where dawn is darker than night itself, and morning darker than daybreak. This deception of our senses, which makes us pause between night and dawn and between dawn and morning, reveals that familiar city to us, the city we could never see before this moment, for neither in our waking hours nor in our dreams have we ever visited this corner of the world. We would be perceived as interwoven bodies, leaping dolphin-like out of the sea of the unconscious, our souls huddling on the deep sea bed, interpenetrating each other and continually reliving the impossibility of mutual indistinguishability. Souls embedded in the this-way and the that-way current, whose anchor holds more strongly than stasis to the edge of the sea and the edge of the land are become body and soul truly only by means each of the other. The deception of our senses would lead us to perceive that the world, like love, rocks spring and autumn this way and that, between tenderness and homicide; the deception of our senses would lead us to believe that, like the night's black soot and light's transparent glass, like summer glittering on the water and in the air, like the disappearances into winter's fogs, like the promise borne by a glance deep into the other and the vanity of anticipation, in cold and empty rooms, sinking slowly into the murky grey suffocating foam – all this joy and pain suffuses the body to the very tips of our fingers and toes, and electrifies the surface of our skin. The deception of our senses seems to establish as fact the material nature of the world and the worldly nature of matter, and with that to establish as fact that not only the earth, not only we ourselves, not only him whom we love, but even that love itself is created by God. All this deception of our senses occurs because in our worldly life we are unable to imagine death, whether it be death of the body or death of the soul, or whether it be the rapturous conjoining of the two, or the consensual agreement between the living, the rapturous world-creating strength of two gazes each deepening into the other. Both the failure to understand and the failure to withstand our existence are born of the deception of our senses which leads us to a concept of death penetrating the parts of our body, revealing itself to be itself a part of our life, a molecular splinter from material structure, the shadow cast by an illuminating destiny. Thus it becomes understandable and withstandable; that is to say its essence, which is indeed the failure to understand and withstand, remains hidden, until we can perceive its own opposite, nothingness, the darkness beside the light, beneath the light, surrounding the light, as chaos surrounds order, as flowers bloom around twisted decaying creepers, surrounded by marshfire, an image of hell reminding us of the pain of our life. And *we see those who were killed, who lie in coffins,* like those *about whom you remember never more because they are separated from your hands.* We see this as if God is turning his back on us – not as if in his absence – the insanity of presence and abandonment separated the one from the other and yet co-existing.

There are in this pain of insanity proofs of the non-existence of God so tortuous that the Devil alone would be capable of conceiving them – the Devil whose own existence proves the existence of God. The source of the deception of the senses, continually revolving vision and illusion as each becomes the one the other, is simply this very absence, an absence which, here in this railway station concourse, is as vivid as only a vision can be, which makes the fact of your existence and that you once embraced me as unlikely as the unlikely yet actual pigeons flying to and fro through the holes in the walls which are made not of bricks but of cold and darkness.

Were the existence of God established, then the existence of these pigeons would be established too, and not only their circling between inside and outside, between light and dark, between atmosphere and nothingness, on routes as undefinable as space itself and this very place. There would be wings – the essence of their existence. Then we would find ourselves gently eased into an understanding of how the intricate cells of the feathers enclose the air. We would find ourselves gently eased into the reality of this understanding of the transcendant rational structure of the air itself, the creation of a perfect balance between weight and weightlessness, between solidity and insubstantiality, the differing thermal expansions of matter. Then we would arrive at the certainty that these winged souls were indeed pigeons, or some other, unknown, never previously observed and never previously observable birds, the vibrating fragments of dream and illusion which accidentally and randomly most closely resemble pigeons, which have established a pigeon-ness because we named them or perceived of them as pigeons. And the non-existence of God would provide our certainty. In that event we should never question whether this part of the day is dawn or morning, this part of the day which transports us between the past and the future, because neither past nor future time would exist; there would be a continuous permanent present, a frozen, motionless silence unbroken by unquenchable waves caused by the splashing of creation in an ocean of emptiness. And if the absence of one single man were to awake resounding words of woe from the innumerable corners of the world, then our pain would grasp, as now it does not, at only one being between the murmuring waves breaking and pulling back again and again from the rocks on the shore. We would not weep at the same moment for him who died, or for him who killed us, choosing in the place of our death his own life, or for him who accepted our unchanging love throughout the decades and who refused the promise of the ecstasy of our single hour. If the sense of deception and betrayal we felt for all of these were not to fill our cup of bitterness to the brim, how could we love them all as if they were one single entity, how could we grieve for them all as if they were one single entity, and how could we feel ourselves eternal and unimaginable, that one absence embodied in our longing for them all? If we could not experience the intensity of joy and sorrow in the bidding of farewell, in that sense of the world being universally present – even within ourselves – how else might we learn through the longing for that absent world the eternal intermeshing of presence and absence? And if we were not to have learned the final poignancy of leave-taking and the intimacy of union beyond death, how could we endure, through year upon year, the renewed circulation of plant life's bitter sap, the anguish of the burgeoning bud and of birth deeper than any leave-taking. These are pains whose bright light renders them indistinguishable not only from joy, but from devotion. If we were not to have learned to distinguish the abyss separating night and dawn and the abyss separating dawn and morning, how could we experience the continuity of time which obliterates these transitions? And if we were not to have been certain that the blackness melting in the passage from night to dawn is no different from the chilling of the winter dawn into the darkness of the winter morning, how could we then differentiate between the click of the footfalls across this station concourse and the metal clank of the buffers. And if the certainty of the existence of God were not to dissipate as the dawn wind, leaving the impenetrable chill of his absence, how then could we withstand the dark night within our own souls, the intermeshing of existence and non-existence within our own souls, where the only sound, deep in the depths of our anxiety, is the chord of courage, a chord on which may be made the music, in an immeasurably and timelessly brief moment between dawn and morning, fixed eternally to this single point of space between the soul and the invisible wall of the icy air, of God's name.

BETWEEN

Autumn and Winter

A few days ago there were russet-red leaves scuttering between the poplars and the hedge facing them, between the stone walls and through the arched gate where the wind gathers and thickens and cannot drive itself through the narrow mesh of the lattice of the branches. The glistening palm-shaped leaves of the wild grape still adorned the warm porous stone. The large shining walls reminded me of those cold mornings before we first met, before the brilliant explosion of the dawn of love; tongues of flame re-create the wonder of that dream, once hidden, now rich with meaning, an expression of the thoughts that then, long since, I dared not explain. Leaves falling and falling from the ever more naked trees, traversing nature, hesitant and now, now they are nothing. If I should look up out of the high kitchen window, in the branches of the walnut tree opposite I can see the random and yet geometrically rigid beauty of their twists and turns – a beauty for which it would be wrong to use the words appropriate to the *other* – the illusion of leaves caught in the play of light between light and shade. This is one of those mysteriously sad days that nature creates and on which the word 'season' bears another meaning, a changing of time, and passing before or a passing beyond, rather than simply the transition from autumn to winter. Within the soul in which the shift from autumn to winter implies the torturing agony of love for one who lives and the icy solidity of love for one who is dead, two differing conditions reveal themselves, not divided by days and hours as are the conditions of nature. And although they may not exist simultaneously, yet through the disparateness of time they bear witness to the unbearable disparateness of this our sole existence. The air is capable of holding within itself fragmentary motes without dissolving them into itself and maintaining their individual physical qualities – solid matter within gas; carbon, silicon, pollen mixed and held within oxygen and nitrogen – and not only their physical qualities but their metaphysical qualities – light, wave motion, uncontainable stardust. This other element permeates our world and here and there we may perceive it twinkling through the fraying tapestry of physical matter. It constantly reappears within our soul, a love unified in its illusion, a reality of images approaching the visual accuracy of photography, the evaporation of the material world, an answering gesture or merely a sigh, an unexpected glance, opposing positions on a chessboard, illegal moves at first sight seeming legal, momentary warmth in the cold air scarcely causing the naked branches the slightest movement, the reality of leaves now distantly past, or the obverse, a momentary chill in warm air. This disturbing disparateness, which, taking the form of despair, smuggles death into life – at a point where the word 'complete' may still stand in antithesis to 'death' – crowns itself with wonder just as the summer tree is crowned with a halo of sunlight. Wonder, unified, yet maintains this distinction, as does hope, and thus are the threads of our own and another's life woven into a single fabric that covers the future with the reality of hopelessness.

The tragedy played out on the stage of time present seems not only imbued with wonder because nature yields itself up to a greater power, the power of destruction – which itself is also a function of nature, and not only in the same way that life is a function of sleep, its natural other half; and not only in the same way that sleep is a function of death, which feeds it in the same way that the sea feeds the waters of the island lake – and not only because death exists in a vast and inconceivable span of time, a function of resurrection, of which it is both a constituent part and against which it stands in opposition. As death disappears, so it yields itself up to reawakening; that which died should never rise again – and again and again. Those born to a new life in this world are those who have already endured the agony of death in an old life – an agony that contains within itself both the knowledge of the impossibility of continuation and the knowledge of the impossibility of resurrection. This seems miraculous as with it the very essence of time itself – event and passage – imply an eternal recurrence beyond event and passage; time itself is breaking down the walls of time's labyrinth. This translates that which is inconceivable and unimaginable within our consciousness into the conceivable and imaginable – something alien to our consciousness. It creates within our very selves a consciousness beyond existence, earths within us the lightning bolts of hope and hopelessness and thus imbues our existence with the fragrance permeating from spheres beyond our existence, the fragrance of spheres between autumn and winter.

But what is this fragrance, wafting into nothingness, into time without time, which did not arise from material reality, not from birth and not from death, which is not the time of passing, and also not from the seasons, nor from that small proportion of this earth covered with fertile soil, with fruit and the fresh lattice of the trees, nor from that segment of the sky filled with stars? This small corner of the world, this quadrant of a circle, which memories fold in on themselves and sink deep into the well of the past, reveal the entirety beneath the surface, the plenitude of the instant before it brims over, and on its spherical surface, where a myriad solstices collapse each into the other, a mirror of the future. But beyond the knife-blade fissure in the surface of time is hermetic time, which cannot be separated from existence or from non-existence – both engendered by the material world – and it is for this very reason that it cannot preserve the childhood image of the grape or the apple, the image of the high-ceilinged room filled with old brown furniture, or the dark purple stubble with the lilac-edged clouds; the fragrant exhalation of the musty earth, the fog, the light prickling of fine drops of rain, the bluish aura of first snow, the virginal hot-cold knee-high snow as yet untrodden on the banks of the freshly frozen river at the winter solstice at the turning of the year. It cannot restore, not even in memory, that quiver of terrifying, bewitching happiness, nor the anguish that pulls us down into the oozing mud, nor the manic energy of liberated desire like the scurrying paws of tiny rodents. It cannot resurrect life once the axe blow of death has severed autumn and winter, against which continuity may not stand, whose barrenness reveals this odourless, colourless, soundless non-existence, a slowly spreading grey mildew, dissolving, softening, melting into the muddy pool of all that has gone before and which yet now, in the deep red heat of pain, bears witness to previous existence.

We cannot know, because its depths cannot be sounded, whether this fresh, swiftly deepening chasm of time is simply our own headlong fall into the defining instant of rupture between autumn and winter, the agony of being torn from reality, our own inner death mirroring the death of the world, or the world fissure consequent on the ripping out of the soul. We do not know whether here on the dividing line between time and timelessness we relive again and again the final disappearance of autumn, still teeming with life, cracking walnuts on the ever-shady moss-covered stone steps, moisture oozing through the veins of leaves, sluggishly wasting and bleaching foliage, the parching of grasses, the

petals of tiny poisonous flowers changing hue, from green to its oppo-
site, red, and to yellow and brown, the browning of red silk, these
perverse and alienating metamorphoses that yet, even in their final
moments, bear witness to the fullness and sweetness of life, even if that
sweetness is the sweetness of decay, bearing the sweet apple smell of
putrefying fruit. Shall we then bid farewell to life? There was a time when
I awoke to joy every day every dawn that he was alive, he whose soul has
already marched down the brimstone road of death's agony, he whom I
abandoned, such was the illusion of my own false joy, to tread the stony
path of loneliness; yet in this joy I embraced him and bore him over the
threshold, which once crossed sealed him into death and clothed me in
the dust of life, his escort, and aboard the sinister barge. Did I seek to
accompany him only so far as the jetty, that vivid reminder of the banally
familiar: the pink house, a dam with a road beside it, the sweeping course
of the river? The landscape on both sides of the river was saturated with
joy and we were able to lean over the water for two hours together – the
richest hours of my life – holding each other's hands with the gentlest of
active pressures and the smoothest of passive caresses, our fingers inter-
twined, living still within the illusion of autumn, still within this life,
even if the autumn and the intertwining had already leaped over to the
chill far bank of winter. Since then I no longer know whether it was I
alone, or both of us together, whether it is always the same autumn, the
season of our parting, or earlier autumns which nurtured and fore-
shadowed this final autumn. Do we still inhabit this same autumn, which
belongs finally and eternally to loneliness, like Nansen's endless march
through uncharted Greenland, day after day facing the fear of death by
cold, in the indivisibility of isolation and comfortable union, in the hair-
fine fissure between the ice membrane and the earth's glowing core
which is the dwelling place of God.

The dwelling place of God may be conceived only as a place filled
with itself waiting to be filled, a place where a heart brimming with love
and pain, flooding outwards and absorbing inwards, crawls towards that
which is non-existent, where the void itself is but an illusion, where there
is only consciousness, where there is no fissure between the dual condi-
tions of actuality, its invisible reality outside space and its eternity out-
side time. If we ever attain that condition where we are able to conceive
of his presence, he whose existence is beyond contemporary reality and
whose eternity is beyond the concept of endlessness. Thus, the pain of

our life, rooted as it is in space and time and growing from the pain of space and time, may transcend a form of existence inconceivable in terms of existence, not even its own opposite, a form created out of existence and pain, which embraces and contains all pain rooted in existence and thus in space and time. In the same way we can conceive the mystery of the shift from autumn to winter as mirroring the mystery of the shift from life to death. It is an image of the invisible and inconceivable quest for transformation, the quest we can sense only in the created images of an indefinable past and an unascertainable future, melded in a non-existing instant of the present, between evening and night, between dawn and morning, within the fissure that is not between the void and the material, the twin conditions of a higher reality. An existence beyond the memory of leaves caught by the wind and the image of naked branches suddenly breaks free from memory and meaning itself, in the same way that an ancient love and its pain, the trembling of the heart and the heart itself, at the same time breaks free from itself and from the world, away from the object of desire and the one who sought to love, and all that pain, through which existence took form and substance and life, as between autumn and winter the actuality of death slides into non-existence.

Can there be anything more actual than this journey slipping from afternoon into dusk, beneath an overcast sky, as the sun occasionally breaks through the low cloud cover, but not on the far icy bank? Beyond where our soul transcends itself, in the intensifying penetrating light of an ultra-violet or infra-red brilliance, the sun stands within a static void. It makes no attempt to penetrate the incomparable light of an identical wavelength but of another element produced by this void. Can there be anything more actual than this selfsame sun, which sometimes appears in the guise of a moon, made visible on a wintry afternoon, seemingly a metal disc apparently illuminated by its own infinitely distant strangeness? No, now it appears like some weighty golden globe floating above the soft grey clouds dense with snow and as it slowly sinks towards the horizon's edge, revealing itself intermittently and in those instants, in the glittering icy light that cannot melt the cold of the void, as if it were the Godhead maintaining life itself, or the emblem of that Godhead, an emblem bearing a value identical to itself. Can there be anything more actual than the endless transmutation of ourselves from instant to instant, inflaming and incinerating our existence, anything more actual than the incandescent yet fading greenness of the familiar flatlands, than a few trees misleadingly resembling the isolated copses and spinneys of our old familiar road? Slowly in that union in which I exist only conjoined with absence, this negative world of absence almost as familiar as the old trees if not more familiar, because this endless journey in its own particular way, like the icily silvered and wearily golden sun, freezes his present into me and melts me into his frozen non-existence. Is this more actual than this journey between a higher and a lower reality, the migration route of living souls into the country of the dead far beneath the earth, whose border gates I approach with a slow, dignified, sacrificial march? Yet in the end I stumble over those who have been abandoned on the leaden tomb-like darkness of the rough, muddy path, the sudden currents of icy air in the wind borne from the openness of some unknown parkland; stain-like shadows fly up from the airy nests of densely packed dunes and hillocks with sinister beating wings into the darkness of the bushes and the yet deeper darkness above the overgrown meadows and the worn gravestones. Is this more actual than the road that soon reaches its ending and yet goes on for ever? Colours disappear into the clouded darkness and the impenetrable blind dark, between late afternoon and evening and already one with night, on the border of autumn and winter, in the place where the world of the living and the world of the dead abut. Is it more actual than the flame of the oil lamp, which I, sobbing violently, try to keep alight in the teeth of the gale, as if this warm golden light shining in the darkness would fix my memories and my ability to remember to the cold earth of your burial mound? It gutters and fails again and again. Is it more actual that the flame that will not light?

So is it more actual than the light of the non-existent flame, than the wind, the gusts, that again and again extinguish that flame as it again and again rekindles? More actual than the wind which is an eternal mystery, the movement of a void, which cries out for air or for the soul between layers of disparate gases, from secret vents, behind which we imagine ever more secret nests – the existing and the non-existing forms of reality approaching an imitation of the certainty of reality – from where fly skywards invisible birds, the beating of their wings making the flame upon your grave gutter, birds that rest upon the air yet also cause to move this selfsame air, themselves creating currents and these currents buoying them upwards, the current they themselves created and to which they must entrust themselves. The heart that engenders pain, which frees itself, is swept away on its own waves into the same dark of secret oceans as the twilight by the river bank, in the late afternoon and evening, between the clouded blue of the sky and the blind darkness of the air, the candlelit warmth of life and the eternal lingering continual dying, stirring, surviving. This anguish, from some unfathomed distance, continually extinguishes and rekindles the flame on your burial mound, the non-igniting, wind-buffeted flame of the oil lamp, this flame echoed in the starry sky and the water mirroring that sky, the muddy pools in the grave pits like soot-filled lagoons, all gathering reflected light, flickering in these mirroring surfaces as long as there exist in this world mirroring surfaces, mirroring water and mirroring sky, stars down below and stars up above, stars within the heart, the heart that even now desires its own pain, seeks it drunkenly from the cold, from the night, from loneliness and in the wild-geese cries of passing death, intoxicated by the endless flatlands and the lacy network of Venetian waterways flowing into mourning and hopelessness, from the dual, mirrored love of the grave flame, from the cold mirror image of embers glowing bright again in the gusts of wind blowing from beyond reality. Is there another truth between autumn and winter to be inserted into our existence, like the pain within the heart?

Is there anything more actual than the countless transformations of our material world, now that we have slowly crossed the bridge and passed from one riverbank to another, from autumn into winter, our bodies and the air both colder now with the weight of the far side which drags our steps, so that finally this future without time without space is slowed infinitely into the present and the instant presumed to be final jolts into an eternity where once there were crimson leaves and now white phantom shadows flicker, where once there were entwining vines and grass stalks and wild forest flowers, and now there are the dazzling stars of crystallized frost and surprising vistas through the hills mingling with other images of the world – with the exception of that one city's mirror glitter – which inspire in us an emotion beyond sight, plunging us into the spiral vortex of death, the unconscionably swift fall from the sickly warmth of autumnal decay into the frozen lifelessness of winter. The death of the human soul at this time is revealed as its own image on the rainbow surface of this illusory world. The vision – what may be conjured by a single word – destiny: on one hand fathomless distance separating the opaque depth of our existence from the patent reality of its apparentness, so that whoever lives, if able to answer the question on death's actualness, a form for ever unknowable, not that it is possible to refer to the concept of reality and carry meaning, or that we cannot imagine the windy hilly roads of our life approaching their destination; and on the other hand reaching out again and again in our pain, comparable to the agony of absence, resembling reality, dispensing with the actuality of truth within the mirror play of non-existent reality, the suffering heart crumbling to dust.

Long ago, faded now from memory, bleached from the world, the fiery red leaves on the hedge of the opposite house, the lattice of the branches of its walnut tree, the cracking of its bony brown knuckles, patterned like skin stretched across a skull, every time seemingly the last, and yet every time awakening the hope that stirs even after the very last time, the hope that autumn will not die. This blind hope contains a faith beyond the persuasions of the frosted bushes and the layer of snow that the line between autumn and winter is fine indeed, as fine as the line between memory and oblivion, as light as the line between love and emotion, crawls into the fissure, into the vortex of darkness between autumn and winter, and guides me – or am I pushed? – into the same vertiginous fall, spinning, fearing, hoping for myself the single thud at the unattainable bottom of the well. I shall never know whether it is attraction or repulsion that reveals to me the fissure between autumn and winter. How should I know which element in my falling allows me to perceive the two as one; not human faces, human gestures, not the essence of souls granted by God, but actually through the forces themselves of attraction and repulsion, the real and the beyond real, because perhaps the law of gravity that pulls our existence into the centre of the chasm of our existence through all the fissures of the world is no less than the extinguishing of the flame, of visible and invisible darkness, their mutuality beyond any distinction of life or death.

BETWEEN

Dying and Death

The patient is just slipping into bed, they have just covered the patient or helped her into a white dressing gown, which they drape round her still-living body day after day as it slowly shifts towards invisibility, as the skin becomes ever more smooth and transparent, a body that was once so delightfully graceful, light, airily evanescent, but now all that remains is a hair-fine relief on the pillow and the sheet, or to be more precise between the sheet and the coverlet, which, in her agony, the patient's arms, twitching, thrashing, have tried to throw off, or, so far as movement in her legs is still possible, to kick off, for now there is even less strength than there was only a few days ago, strength to ask us again and again to remove her bedclothes, to help her sit up, to help her turn over, the which wearily we did, with ever increasing weariness and impatience because in some way we did not trust the ignorance within helplessness, the desire to be free of the weight of bedclothes, nor the actuality of being sat up, for before another three minutes have passed, she is asking to be laid down again, and by this time we are staggering with tiredness, our limbs are leaden and at this time we begin to become angry because our tiredness is hollow and futile, as we collapse into this hollow, futile tiredness. And yet we rejoice in this tiredness, the leaden weariness which we must conquer again and again in the instant of every movement, because we are maddened by the shame of sitting here, healthy and clean, our bodies feeling good, clothed in the health of our own bodies, in fragrant, clean clothing, and because we cannot free ourselves, not for one single instant, from the hideous, from the inconceivable, because of that maddening distinction between us, because of the pain, powerful as an arc light, flashing between death lurking in this still living body and our own indifference. The near physicality of this pain burns bright like an everlasting bulb, never truly embodied, simply a mirror image or – and this is worse – the embodied image of the desire for pain. Why did it seem to us unbearable, this bodily agony, an agony that was not ours to feel and yet that was agonizing precisely because it was not ours to feel, that this unsensed sensation assumes the guise of pain, as if we were to experience a compassion for a pain unperceivably distant from us, far on the glaciers of infidelity and abandonment, in the distinctiveness of the shadowlands of disloyalty and abandonment?

This gulf around us existed both within ourselves and outside ourselves. It was not affection; it was not growing familiarity or the ties of blood; it was not fear of our own pain to come, but it was he himself, moving within us, within me, flowing with my blood, as I became a mother in this pain, because I was in labour, although my pains were less than his for he, bathed in blood and sweat, was giving birth to his own death, as I was giving birth to my own baby sister, as though this was my own child, that I should now endure in innocence her death and hence the bitter death of my own child, a death prefigured in birth. This grief falls short of every other mourning, every other bereavement, every other abandonment, because it is only with this act that I could experience the pain that measured the pain of the other, the pain of the actual mother and the actual child, who were experiencing the obliteration of their own origins, their own source, as life guttered and turned slowly to ashes, within the body which has almost become one with the bedclothes, infiltrating the linen and the cotton, the bandages of the dead, existing now where all there is is the actuality of the instant, a presence perceivable only by others and the absolute unity of inner endurance, where there is now no faith, no trust, no affection, no continuing God, no and not even myself, but in the place of the everything that is exceeded by all earthly measures, in this non-perceivable actuality, there is the unrecorded existence of body and soul, which is simply pain, and we are as incriminated as Isaac in the instant where eternity is found, in the sweat of agony, in the gateway at the indistinguishable point between life and death, at the threshold of our blind and dark liberation.

How may we survive that other death, one yet more terrifying than this, because it does not come to an end in the very last instant, but is a continuity of death, with its concomittant fear, and defencelessness, but above all helplessness, disguised in images not of death but of the eternally approaching, of the infinitely horrifying, for there in the midst of the deeply frightening, the deeply threatening, exists an enforced silence, because it is eternally forbidden to speak of this, because in its kinship with muteness lies the very identity of pain, and yet this comprises something utterly different from the pain of one who is isolated, who declares that without that that we, we who listen, in all our lived and relived pain, we would then arrive at a true understanding and not for one single instant longer could we then bear to sit beside the sickbed, our faces suffused with the deceitful smile of a willingness to help, but neither would we be able to stand and leave, because we would be carrying with us the pain of that person and shame would shackle our feet, the anguish of our shame would nail our feet to the floor of the hospital corridor. And so we would slip away down corridors whose ceramic tiles are smeared with mucus, stinking and filthy, into dimly lit courtyards leading off one another, and into the now dark and empty night where all that we can hear is the clicking of our own heels. We are cowards for taking flight, for that option seeming the lesser anguish than sitting here at the bedside, by a consciousness on the edge of extinction, cooling, cooling, shut in on itself, never reaching us, going before and yet – perhaps certainly – engaging with its own pain, and this consciousness, like some small rodent spinning in its treadmill, ever and again taking on itself the pain of the world. It takes on itself the pain of the world which now has a greater truth for her than that other truth which obliges her body to dissipate imperceptibly into the wrinkled sheets, as her limbs twitch and spasm, and her pain, in its leaden casing, is now unreachable by the drugs whose poison saturates her flesh, saturates every cell, mangles the walls of cells and the networks and membranes of her tissues. How may this dying more hideous than death be lived through, this process which embraces more despair than that instant followed by nothingness? Because nothingness itself is not actual and yet this process, which it utterly other than what we commonly perceive as the actual, is incomparably more actual, because what finally could be more actual than the pain that twists and tunnels within our bones, giving a birth to our life? What could create our life if not that power which, removed from the images of the outer world, projects images and sounds into that outer world which is, in fact, the projection of our inner selves? It is both a projection and an embossing, and it is our illusion too, because how could it be possible to survive the deceit of our senses of this floating existence and non-existence between life and death, which in the manner of a Moebius strip connects on both the inside and the outside. What emanated from the outside and impinges from the outside is nothing but the deformed projection of the view from within and what directs us from within, a secret embedded in a muddy ditch, a hidden pebble allowing destiny to flow around it, a destiny formed of its own stony existence, a destiny of non-confession, of a false turning aside, determined by the same laws, whether it be that the stars of the upper sky or the stars of the lower sky marshalled our steps through the upper world or the lower world, through the insoluble labyrinth of God, the labyrinth which is God himself, a labyrinth whose paths follow the antithetical direction from the direction of the clock hands of God.

Would I have suffered this dying in the same manner, would I have plunged into the agony of the being who once stood closest to me – not by the right of blood, nor through the inheritance of common genes, but by the rights invested in the milk we both sucked from the breast of the identical mother – she who not only stood closest to me, almost within the same shared identity, because we were rooted in some unnameable deep, grown from the identical soil, soil from which identical stalks would shoot, the double stem of two siblings? Their commonality is rooted so deep, where no ray of the sun may penetrate, yet bearing witness through an imprinting of the soil of an ancient sun. Would I have plunged into the agony of the being bound to me throughout life by tangled jealousies, envies, wilful and unwilling turnings aside and a yet to be fathomed consciousness? We were bound together by the differences of our nature and our destiny – for the silk cocoons of love are woven not only from understanding and goodwill but from an infinitely more mysterious thread, whose tensile strength withstands all opposed resistance. Would I have lived through this suffering if I were not to be living and dying my identical destiny within her destiny, both of us living out the destiny of our immediate parents and in their destinies the pasts of our ancestors, whose mesh of shoots and roots engulfs this planet and whose fine root threads demonstrate that in the distinction of difference we two recognize each the other, with a sense, unknown, inexplicable, for herein lies the principal proof that our consciousness springs from the depths, in which every pain and every fragment of human understanding experienced by our ancestors is melded together; whether I would have lived through her death with her, in the same manner, if this particular death, not the ancient death, not the death of the other, the death we truly live together, the birth hidden in our birth, the humiliation of the death of our life. These are links in the selfsame chain that connect the two births and the two deaths, that of the

mother and that of the child, loss and discovery, generation upon gener-
ation of freshly child-bearing mothers, whose child-bearing is loss and
whose children freed into the world live through the sundering, both at
the same time and not together, loving in closer formation, as the moon
and the sea, as the high tide and the low tide on a moonlit night, at once
waxing and waning, eternally both within and without, the intensity of
actual being and the sense of non-existence beyond the human, a pre-
human void, the certainty of our existence eternally lost in time, yet not
in the past, which is utter death, but in our own birth, our own children,
the death of our own mother, yet not in the future, the continuity of our
existence ensured with any child, but within an instant, in that which is
tangible to us, touch, smell, hearing, and indeed sight, we discover the
unbearable as we have no sensory organs capable of perceiving with
intensity, of sensing the material and the immaterial on this Moebius
strip, the images of images, the intermingling colours indistinct, the
shapes perceived by our vision undefined, structured only by the illusion
we carry within us of the curved and the malleable, transformed within
our own eyes, themselves rainbows cast on the membranes of the transi-
tory, themselves paintings stretched on the world-frame. Why is one
death transformed into your death, and your death into the disappear-
ance of another, why transformed into that particular one, whom the
waves and years of defeat carry ever further away, to an unperceivable
life, death and yet not quite death? The absence of the certainty of life
lived at one particular instant, the fragrance of a soft frail body, as
gloomy legends journey into the sunset in a garden of golden apples, is
now closer than she who departed long since, she whose love suffocated
into ashes, floating with green leaves through the air, untouched by cold,
shaded from the sun's shining by the chill embracing those who are dead
and will now never rise again, because there is no longer a country to
return to, in ruins the houses in which they lived, the gardens and wood-
lands which occupied their visits, these outer spaces filling the inner
spaces and not returning, those buried in the labyrinth where the paths
run on different levels, and thus all space disappears from my life and
time withdraws into itself, and thus the harsh gritty river bed runs dry,
and time which once heaved and rumbled in its tortuous existence,
embracing death and love, darkness and the deep that glistens and glows
invisibly like the paddle-wheel driving the waves, but where flows the
past river in which both dissolved together within me, filling me with

belief, and where is that life which, like metal, glittered darkly, a shower of powder, searching among the rocks, searching out a route for cascading water, which flows from fresh heights to fresh depths, forming momentary lakes; where is that water, the water of my life, in which the stars bathed with the pebbles rolling beneath them, which flowed onwards, carrying earth, branches, leaves and bones with it, which breathed into itself the air from the sky and the dense mud, the gritty streams now gone, swallowed into the graves, vanishing into the graves, never to re-emerge as a hidden stream as the graves of the depth have themselves now disappeared and into which graves I too disappeared, so that in their death, as it were an immersion into the baptizing Jordan waters, should arise new life on earth, which from the desert of our non-existence God slowly metamorphoses the labyrinthine forest into a second place of unknowable location in the unrecognizable place of our death. The burial, a mere symbol, with a woven poem of regular stanzas here and there breaking through a line of pine trees and crowning foliage, and the occasional cypress, here, the autumnal sky clouded and the muddied leaves brushing the earth. We become creatures of the earth ourselves, losing our trust in that which separates us, living within ourselves, and that unforgettable image imprinted within us, the photographed graves, the browns, the greens, the sun-baked golden yellows, as we lay beneath a mound of earth, so close was that time when that body, that body from my body, was 'returned to the earth from which it came' and did not die once more, the earth the mother, but granted there my body, weighted down with earth, intoxicated with happiness, as the grail guarding the miracle, a body not born of bodily flesh, of the ecstasy contrasting with the bodily shame of two bodies, from a knowledge of sin, and haste, and exile, of commonly created humiliation, but rather of the emotion that embraced within itself the sky and the earth and with which the sky and the earth subsequently formed a unity, which in isolation was enough to ask of God the miracle of burial. Whether there are truly children to whom the angel did not give news of the life to come and for whom not-Gabriel stands in the doorway, spreading his wings in front of the window, in his room in the rosy glow of dawn, beneath the stars' lazy light and the gold-embossed firmament announces that the angel fathered these children and we should see them as wonderful, sent by another world, their bodily actuality not physical as if born of the body, but inexplicably of the soul, attracted towards another soul by a power stronger than physical power, and thus are our bodies locked within the instant of two bodies united in liberating mutual immersion, splitting between the pressure of the bodies, returning into disembodiedness, lawfully and naturally, still glistening rosy red, dusted with the stardust that shines through the translucence of human skin, as if to dull the sparkling in that place where there is no earth, no mud, no autumn leaves, no bubbling sounds from the stream, however the weeping of a child creates an un-understood counterpoint, the flooded forest not sounding like the shuffling of aged feet and in the candlelit cemetery, beneath the glittering dome of light, into that village graveyard where I so often came with that person who is now but earth, a memory, a memory not passing into memory, a memory of existence, an existence of earth, water, the river and smoke, the autumn quinces and the burning wood spiced with the fragrance of actuality, an actuality that was death too, a 'from earth we came and to earth shall return', an actuality that is the unbearableness of pain, bloodily dismembered flesh, cold tears and the graveyard, where together we stood by the gravestone beneath which lay the bones of a tiny body, not as now with all who rest here, the memories of themselves, one among all these, a symbolized soul, passing the symbolic actuality of existence that it now itself symbolizes, not material actuality, and not pain more actual than any other element, but among such pain which, slowing and slowing, divides existence from life itself.

We left the graveyard, behind us leaves tangled with creepers, the richly veined marble bearing Hebrew letters, the arched tombstones and the black marble tombs all now forgotten, once emblems of completed lives, something utterly other, the name perhaps hiding unnameable pain and suffering, names standing for memories, which now may not be recalled, the naming of these graves, of these souls, who sleep, dreaming we know not what of, dreams incapable of encapsulating things of the earth. We grasp those things that are hard, those things that are malleable, in this twilight, as the world separates from its essence and colours dissolve into a greyness that is indistinguishable from whiteness and from softness and from the stillness of sorrow, which is tinged at the same time with the sweet and with the unbearable, so that we crave it, a gentler death, a death whose enchanting magic touches us, itself a reality, half a reality, perhaps more true than sight, than emotion and sensation, in our eyes, in our ears, taking form and substance in our vision. Why does it bring such pain? Clothed now in their dead dust, they may not be understood by us as dead, because in their living lives their words were not understood, they who lie here, their bodies mouldering and crumbling, in hope of personal resurrection, the gravestones bearing witness to their hope of personal resurrection, the stone crosses and the crumbling limestone winged angels, angels of another world, a second death entering the coffin we pull tight around ourselves, from the instant of our birth to the instant of our death, for there is nothing else to create the illusion of understanding, or the inexplicable condition of love, and the plant, the creeper, that winds its way into the soul, to flower in secret when near to death, reaching roots down into the waters of death, like a waterlily with exquisitely fragile petals, beyond number, coloured buds, leaves, like a cutting from a horse chestnut tree, chilled by winter, as customary in mid-January, the time of deception, warmed and protected in its pot, like some wondrous orchid creating an ever greater wonder in our eyes from the instant of creation to the instant of renewed wonder, the single story, born of God's incomprehensible idea to renew creation out of the waters of death, from the muddy October earth, mingled soil and water, the foundations of a city beyond measure, at least beyond measure in human terms, in which there are no wooden stakes, no islands of crumbling sandstone, crumbling limestone, but whose palaces are built of pulsing and vibrating columns of love, radiating love. If we do not know this, if we do not speak of this with respect, we shall be exiled from here, unlived destinies slowly atrophying, faithless, abandoned within ourselves in a deprived deathly void, an apparent orphanhood, and yet shining on them still, like one final ray of sunlight, the golden beam of our one-time love, the final message to the world from the non-existing sun and the non-existing moon.

And as for me, let me now start, leaving behind the stones in the warp and weft of the light, the muddy paths, indistinguishable from old, muddy, parkland paths, grottoes overgrown with ivy, where I united with the one I now leave here for ever, in death, in ambiguity, forever transformed and absence will no longer mean the dawn of eternally renewed pain. In truth it will not be long before I too lie here, metamorphosing into mud, mulch and decay, in this concrete mapped destiny of physical decomposition, in the suffering of renewing nightmare, like the one I loved more than any other, who is transformed here into mere matter, the slanted, fallen gravestone, the decaying leafmould whispering, the water and rain humming, and the pink chain of past instants, which even in their present times were already symbolic of a disappeared past, for what was this dual life of ours, if not a single farewell extending from the first instant to the last, to that most painful moment, as I threw down that handful of earth, staggering from the sudden realization that now, that even should I fall down beside you, there is no continuance of our dual life, when I lay in your arms, as lying there in your arms I experienced the sin of sorrowless sorrow for the veil of your existence and your non-existence, and so I address the world, like some tightrope walker balanced on a cord between your existence and your non-existence, my own existing and non-existing world. But then you were with me and I was with you until that unspecified day when for once only, until now, I was alone. I did not recognize this instant, because it was not an instant, not part of a thread or continuum of time ticking away, but a completely different winding, convoluted encircling of your life, which stopped me for months afterwards understanding how it was I did not find you in the bed beside me. Again and again the waking was torment, because I always felt as if I was ill, like someone tortured by obsession, because it was not possible for me to be yours for all eternity, because at one time life and death burned within me, and fear, which had frozen solid beneath thickening layers of ice, and love, the presentiment of death, concealed life, which now I know was not death but only a single instant of existence, pure present time, the worldly present and life in its unified unattainability. Yet still there was death and only the continuousness of death, like life itself, both like dragon heads emerging from the depths of the cave, stirring and shivering in our dreams, like that time when you whimpered in your dream, deep in the mud of a dense wood, among the mouldering trees, wading through marshlands pursued by dogs and wild animals, which are gaining on you. I would have understood if your frightened voice did not wake you and I did not wake you either. At such a time, when night's slippery darkness becomes tangible, there was only one time when I did not hear the star-breeze of your breath and then I shifted and stirred beside you, obsessed with you, wanting you to move or wake because of the certainty of the dream, you to live and be beside me, in the warmth of your actuality and the ice-cold sweat of my fear. And now you stir in the icy chill of your actual non-existence and the warmth of the glowing embers of your anguish beyond death, the little flames of deception having burned out and turned to ashes in this heart, between dying and death.

Perhaps he, the other, a stranger to us, is still with us in substance one with death, aiming our steps, the words used for waking us, when for that first time we rose up from the deep dark into the cube of light, the air wild and unknown, among clanking and rattling machinery, for the first time in eternity separate from our mother, who until this moment was both our home and our whole world. And then, some months later, distant from her, on knees and elbows, sliding on our bellies, but always seeking newer and further roads of discovery, crying abandonedly and perversely when checked, knowing ever more surely that our road leads in one single direction, across the gravelly and mossy riverbanks in parkland, with another and alone, advancing towards the sunlit gladed places, as if we, at that time so close to the soil, worming our way towards new shade, would metamorphose into light, take flight with the birds. The dead alone we see now as what moves forwards, until now obliquely, like a magic dowsing rod seeking out gold ore in the ground, towards gold nuggets and granules ablaze with tellurium, God alone knowing of their existence, their glimmer wrapped in darkness, like the blazing of a fire, the broken light turning, as do our faces, seeking the blue veil of the sky, although it is the invisible light and not the rays of the sun that make the sky blue and the sea blue, and colours the murky gloom beneath the trees and the roots deep within the earth, but not the rust red of pain, because invisible light has no colour, indeed it is only they who approach the dead who can tell colour from colour, and perhaps because of this we are profoundly aware of ourselves, concerned with the sight of our own eye, looking, listening to sound, our bodies silent, because we suspect, more truly than the physical substance of the earth, more physically actual than the embodiment of the soul, the body, our existence more actual than death. Because of this we fear to make no record, because our fear of actuality is more than the fear of the torturing wound that wears a mask, of festering ulcers beneath gold and silver, of hair gnawed away by abscesses hidden under exotic hairstyles fastened with a gold pin in a vortex of golden curls. In this carnival our souls hesitate at the turns of staircases in an ancient city, on the point of bridges, in passageways, in the light and the mirroring of water and glass, sinister and beautifully black in the square, which our dual existence may never leave, whether or not this is the existence in which together and within each other we died, now and since the beginning of time, approaching the face of God obscured by the dust of nothingness.

Think of us who lie deep in hollowed graves on the stony hillside, with stone slabs above us, hewed from the same stone as the hill itself. You can see across the graveyard, from one side to the other, there beyond the stone city walls of Jerusalem, but you cannot see through the inconceivable accumulation of graves, which multiply for ever on the same area so that a further receiving place cannot be imagined, yet you see this place, with its unchanging boundaries yet which reach ever wider and you will not be surprised to discover this is another place, free of the side of the hill and the city wall, free of the stones and of the sky, because free of physical matter, occupying this high, fresh ground, this place of God, where the laws are not tangible. Between the graves you seek for the missing ones that once you loved, because they lie elsewhere and far from you, in that country where you visit cemeteries where no limestone slabs cover the limestone-white exposed bones there is earth and leaf-mould and the candle scent of fog and autumn. Candles from All Saints' Day and the withered filaments of rustling rose wreaths protect memories that have themselves metamorphosed into fragrance and silence. The opening doors momentarily stirred for them a present existence, those whose slowly expiring fragrance is evaporating, changing to a silent, slow nothingness as they themselves metamorphose into nothingness. Memories break down into non-existence, and the dead, if they still live, they live in another inconceivable actuality, and left to us only the images, the expanse of the stone graves, encased in the glittering of faith, like a candle flame taking refuge in a wider light, radiating in its hiding place, as they lie hidden in the hope of redemption, under a snow-white sheet of death, they who await resurrection. In pictures of these graves, where the fallen moulder with doubt and knowledge, and in our visions they live there still, they who never received the grace of burial and so who may not look for the resurrection of the body, they who evaporated with burning smoke, in innocence, defenceless, with pain and terror descending into hell, for ever, because of their dread of the immutability of hell, from where the mercy of love may not deliver them. If we see this and know this, and if, in our right minds, we turn to dust down as far as our ankles, then the earth, in the soil of memory past lives crumbling to dust, perhaps alone guards the stirrings of long-gone lives, and whose fragrance alone may wake the memories of the dead. Before the heartbeat's last terrible pulse, will we still have the strength to think of you, for the first time think of you, for whom absence opened the gates to the unbearable absence of God?

I do not know whether or not she escaped towards the thing that ran ahead, its arms making its movements cumbersome, while with my intelligence alone I could not cast off the final rock, but I do not even want to forget the maimed body and its creeping and floundering, its crippled arms and legs and ghostly leaps, its helplessness and obscene twitching. I did not want to unite with what, earlier, years before, had hidden with that, the third figure that grows tall between those in love like a column of smoke. How could we know the third, the other, for me you and for you I, he, with bodiless hands embracing and filling our bodies, so that he is always with the other embraced. Female bodies hold him in their embrace and male bodies waste a myriad myriad lifetimes glittering in his ghostly embrace in a dream in which their existence is non-existent, eternally more actual than every living being. Life itself again and again puts on the disguise of mortality. Truly we would never feel, with the smoothness of our skin, that other mortality wrapped in silk, this cool and clean commencement, stretched out, glistening dully, as if a suspected sun were to rise, on currents of air into the darkened room, on the sea tides of our nights, which not only surround us and sweep us away with them, but dissolve into us, flames inflaming us and flowing out from within us into rooms, like jewelboxes lined with black velvet, while silks gradually form from the glistening of gold. In the anguished gold-loneliness of our autumn afternoons, at that instant when we are most alone, in the absence of a person (for the eternal present of the glittering mirror-deep truth of the now non-existing), being and non-being painfully experienced and then, on the unchartable maps and innumerable clock-tickings shifting into another type of being, incomprehensible and with knife-blade definition, into a tantalizing mystery which now, with the tree leaves of this September dusk, descending, motes and grains of dust catching the slanting light, warmed slowly a little by the sunlight, beyond the beating of the heart and mingled with the substance of instants squeezed within our heart (like sulphuric acid with water, a corrosive bubbling mixing into the till-now mildly warm air) in this warmed September, which even now does not mingle the bright radiance of our childhood with the gloomy, overcast loneliness of our childhood, but not theirs and not ours, the barrier of physical torture, they who fell with hopelessness and our life of the past and in the past united constructs a future, like a tornado of wind or a current of water, lifting sand, uprooted trees, roof-tiles and roof-frames too, homes and lives, all swept away now and for ever. There are shivering souls not dissolving the one into the other, split asunder. Once there was hope of our bodies being completed, an unspoken yearning, a perceived promise arising from our unity with anticipated death. We tremble from birth and in the deathly pressure of love still we seek the intensity of being in love, because the essence of our life past in none other than our escape and our present together, our love tunnelling into death and the endurance of death being buried within love – which in his dying agony was simply unendurable, like the remains of my life – for all this in its unbearableness was forever numbered by eternal unendurable suffering, at the same time as the final smile of the unbroken lighting up of emerging buds. Our escape is fearful silence, with a melody that peters out, as these two forked paths take their separate directions, as we fail in our understanding of God. Sealed within our elapsed lives, is this not what we name as existence separated from God?

BETWEEN

Creation and Birth

If there is no one for me to address, how could I know that there exists one to whom I could address myself? You are the addresser (who in the condition of addressing unites with me, who is addressed). How may I even address him, again and again, as my very addressing would bring him into existence? Is it the same thing if I address him, when I cannot know if I am free from being addressed by him, because if I limit the world into the relation between the addresser and the addressed, or if, on the other hand, I perceive this relation as so infinitely broad that it embraces the entire world? The starry heavens, at which once Abraham gazed in wonder and addressed the Someone, who then for the first time and ever since, and always with this question, precisely with this astonishment, begins to speak, begins to answer. He, the one who was addressed, thus became for ever the one who addressed, and the words used in this addressing, when told and retold, grew as silent as the silence of listening, of muteness, in which the word may be heard, the word that once upon a time was whispered soundlessly across the waters of the lake. This word is different from our word, for if we were to exhale the slowly stilling currents of air and we could then record this sound, black marks on snow-white paper, on winter's virgin snows, as yet untouched by any human step, but his word is neither sound nor symbol, an inaudible resonance and single stroke drawn into nothingness by the arabesques of melody; its medium is nothingness, though it indelibly still derives from something, because nothingness is solely its medium and not its substance. Its substance is invisible: as the air allows light to pass through it, so does this allow itself to be permeated by nothingness. Or a something is passed through a nothing; energy through incomprehensibility. And to demonstrate its physical actuality, it may be perceived as the physical actuality of air permitting the passage of wave particles of light, because energy is not matter; however, in its non-actuality, it is stronger than physical matter, as it indicates it is more constant than physical matter because it holds the essence of physical matter beyond the tendency of all matter to expand. This spiritual truth exists before matter and after matter, oozing below and fluttering above in the mysterious – and for us hopelessly incomprehensible – actuality. That energy is the Word, simply the Word, and above all the Word that created the world, when it was spoken without sound, because there was no air to be its medium, and no living beings to hear and receive the sound.

In that dawn chill, there had already to be a world, because if there had not been a world, how could the word have made a sound? But how could the world have emerged out of the nothingness, if not through words, which formed it together, solidified, drained in a sieve, giving formlessness meaning and through this process form. It was granted the action, the single unrepeatable event, of creation, like the endlessly repeated instant-in-instant continuity of our own creation.

Those words, which create the world again and again, always sound alike. The words come from the near-dark of caves hidden deep within the earth, where the depth itself intensifies so acutely in the wellshafts that the metallic sheet no longer reflects the onyx-black dome of the night sky, this fine, black-lacquered porcelain bowl, but is itself a fragment of it, a repetition of it. It forms a circle, a fragment of the matter that encloses this world of ours without fissure all the night long. It is a part of the darkness, which is itself not the colourless gloom of space but the dense soot or ink of night; it is not the permeable, eternally destroyed and reconstructed soft nothingness constructed of the currents of the wind, but darkness created of nothingness. It became day and night, light and dark, and this darkness is drawn into caves, by the lower world deep within the earth, as it were sea water hiding from the ebb-tide, for with this retention of water the sea does not diminish like the substance of night, drawing dark and water into the pits of these caves, not taking away anything from the outer – more precisely, the upper – darkness, not threatening the cool perfection of night. Such a fragment, like some shard of clay, does not fall to earth from a broken higher substance, into the earth, perhaps through the earth, opening a casement on the opposite surface of the globe, creating a fissure through the impenetrable density, mystical perceiving through the intensity, into these caves of which perhaps churches built by human hands are an upward-reaching echo, an imitation. It is possible that they are neither echoes, nor imitations, but in truth these sky-penetrating buildings are identical to the caves formed like fingers digging deep into the earth. It may be that it is words that create these caves, their own echoes taking on the power of declamation. By the same token it may be that these words are but emblems of these depths. Because man is capable of conceiving upward motion by that which is downward-directed beneath us. So if churches and sanctuaries for those on the run can be perceived again and again in the magic light of their incomprehensibility, as the sometimes visible, sometimes invisible, symbols of this, we cannot conceive of creation by a human soul, that through this sound the human soul was created. If these words can be heard, words that contain a meaning not associated with intelligence, they are like pebbles or like raindrops, the ripples circling ever wider in the human soul. Could it be by chance that we cannot conceive this or suggest a way of making this conceivable in any other way than through the image of water, in the same way that the image of the darkness of night or the darkness of the soul is made concrete for us? Not only because it is visible as opposed to invisible, but because it has substance, as opposed to the concept of insubstantiality, whereas the soul, the breath, the passing life, is nothing but the final single possibility leaving a pale irregular patch of condensation on the cold glass of the mirror. If we are still able to see this lake, as we sense the sound which is the energy of creation even if it does not exist as a word in our language, because perhaps it is music, or something that may not be listened to, the silence of the wind blowing, the stirring in the leaves or the momentary shiver on the surface of a lake, the play of light fragmented, so it is that this black water evokes in us the sense of a soul, of existence, of death, of a formless, infinite, inconceivable everything. If we are unable to conceive of this, how much more impossible the effect of the dropping of pebbles, of jewels, of rain, of the drops of dew rolling down and falling from the tip of the finger of God. These drops are constantly renewed, again and again rising from the depth and radiating in concentric circles, maintaining the truth of the constancy of matter and creating matter that is not subject to earthly measurement, that which only these circular waves, at once confined and radiating, may express as the continuous movement of the lake, resealing at every touch, impenetrable liquid silk dissolving into itself, an unimaginable image of the definition and confinement of our existence.

How can it be conceivable that what moves remains in the same place? That under the falling drop, formed itself of the same matter as the lake, water, or, if other, some pebble or pearl, formed of some other matter, under that drop as it disappears, rings are created on the smooth surface? Not on the surface and not within it either, inner rings hinting at outer rings, with an independent life. Although the lake itself and the rippling rings are indistinguishable, it seems as if they take on different forms of existence. As the rings grow ever wider and further away, the movement, unchanging, not only enshrines their completeness, their closedness, but also their very form, which of all geometrical shapes is the most mysterious. So we recognize its structure as a symbol of perfection throughout thousands of years in the development of our consciousness. It has become a symbol of such potency, continuously radiating and extending, ever newer ripples filling the mass of the matter with which it is identical. Ever identical and ever different because initially it falls from above, from the heights, and we should be unable to discover its location in either the depths or the heights, so that a function of its homogeneity is the inapplicability of the concept of location. At least not in this form, as we perceive our lives broken into colours. We perceive it as the driving force of our eternal urge to wander, the propulsion of our restlessness, which both leads and pushes us, from our very first steps along our winding roads, into the darkness of the night-time forest, across a carpet of pine needles, among the knotted roots winding this way and that across the surface of the earth, in the mystery of fear and terror. In the forest we are deceived again and again by the starry light through the leaves. We arrive at a glade filled with brilliant white moonlight, like a bowl being filled with some unknown, bubbling liquid, its surface lacy, its flavour and substance the coolness of silver, and as we drink we do not know whether it is liquid or light that we sip. The ecstasy its sparkling spreads throughout our limbs diffuses outer strength and inner strength in erstwhile exhausted legs, crouched shoulders and the heart which we believed we could lift up no longer. If we leave this clearing, taking but a single step of a single instant into the moon shadow of the trees, the moon shade, turning back we shall never again find our way through the brushwood, to that circular space that opened momentarily for us. The days of our departure become ever more dreamlike, the place, the boundaries – we were truly there; the magic truly existed. Its vanishing took place within us. As it vanishes it sinks into us, like the silver glades of love in the magic forest of our wandering. Is this not then evidence that the world of substance is something made visible only for us? As colours jostle around us, we stumble to the end of alleyways in cities where among the hundreds of thousands there are only thirty known in total. Here a crossroads emerges, closer to the fearful goal with every step, at the same time yearning to be free of the unbearable weight of the instrument of death, fearing, on arrival, the grasping terror of the unknown horror: not a liberation but an existence more frightening than existing, to which is drawn the bloody sweat of our dying, like darkness falling into the round mirror of the lake, the droplet of dew running down the finger of God, the circles endlessly spreading and incapable of spreading, radiating outwards and yet sealed within themselves, the dying away of the ripples bearing witness to the actuality of the universe not expanding, there being only time, the fallen droplet, the instant of silenced sound, the word leaving the lips of God, the creation of his words, and that it is immaterial whether they signify the creation into existence of our life or of our death.

When the sentence of God, *Let there be light,* was spoken, light erupted into the erstwhile windowless existence, the outlines of objects were drawn, forms appeared giving distinction to the meanings of the world, boundaries were shaped and within this created content, the differentiation of matter, the world came into being: not yet the sea nor the dry land, the sun nor the moon; there were no trees, no plants, no birds nor living beings. There was the single very first action of creation: *and God divided the light from the darkness. And God called the light Day, and the darkness he called Night. And the evening and the morning were the first day.* The first day – and after this came the second day when *God made the firmament and divided the waters which were under the firmament from the waters which were above the firmament.* And then came the third day, when he separated the dry land from the waters of the sea and *the earth brought forth grass, and herb yielding seed after his kind, and the tree yielding fruit, whose seed was in itself* and on the fourth day God created the sun, the moon and the stars *to rule over the day and over the night,* to rule over our soul by day as we emerge into the lightness of the world and separate from the dark which at whatever instant in the beginning of our existence filled our soul with ancient matter resembling the water above which moved the soul of God. And the sun, the moon and the stars separated the light from the darkness. *And God saw that it was good.* And so we must accept the good, accept that our life is divided between day and night, that our understanding is of the day, the waking and the sleeping of the profoundly black formlessness of our emotions changing over time, that this changing, our knowledge, our heart, our sense of wakefulness and relaxation prompting the beating of our heart into an irregular pulse, which God has brought to being with the perfection of every law, in a word creating time, saying, *Let there be lights in the firmament and let them be for signs.* And God created the multitude of animals, with which he populated the earth, and the days and the nights so that there should be those that live, hunt and breed by day and that there should be those whose empire is the darkness of night, the darkness of the soul, that there should be living creatures that have never seen man and that there should be those that live only within us, in that inner darkness, from which the coloured fabric of our dreams are woven, through the insistent sound of the creator's words. And the echoing vibrations guarding the memory of the word, when on the sixth day, God said, *Let us make man in our image, after our likeness,* and with this statement thus finishing the commencement of the world, the process of creation. Evening was brought into being and morning was brought into being and the world was brought into being, created because God declared that man was brought into being *to have dominion over the fish of the sea, and over the fowl of the air, and over every creeping thing that creepeth upon the earth,* that he should have dominion over himself, that he should perceive and take hold of creation, of time, should hear the word that created and continues to create time again and again, the single instant of time, in which there can be no ripple, no froth or spray on the surface of any river at any instant in time. It was not a single drop of water falling into a lake, nor a star chiming its resonant rings in the impenetrable depths, because God did not create that through a word but once the world was born created man in his own image and likeness and the word *was made flesh, and dwelt among us, (and we beheld his glory, the glory as of the only begotten of the Father,) full of grace and truth.*

Thus it was. If time does not dwindle into nothingness, but we imagine it as a river collecting tributaries into itself and flowing out into the sea, then the thought, from that source, emerging into that instant of creation, does not imply a necessity for us to perceive a plane, a parabola, symmetry. If we accept our own part in the suffering of creation, the memory of which, that anguish, the pushing upwards of ragged springs through the earth's hard crust, their bursting through into the air, each layer harder than the previous layer, anguished with streams of water, again and again through this re-formed globe, into these bone-hard boundary walls, in compulsory wanderings, into this exile without knowledge, without even the pain of hopelessness, living streams enduring their terrible exertions. If the two strain against each other and immerse themselves in each other's pain, there we may perceive the agony of God, the agony that no sounding sentences may guide us through, ejected by a single entity, within one single instant. We come to realize that the word of creation is dual, two intertwined with each other, combined with struggling cries of pain: the roar of God, who transformed his own motionless majesty into the eternal transition of eternal truth, who, in the creation of the world, required himself to experience the disorientating shock of his own holiness, the thunder in everything. In some manner the scream of the creature, created not out of the dream, but brought to life from the fissure of nothingness, moist, smeared with the mud of the primordial ooze, bodies tangled with seaweed and creepers, trying to lick themselves, trying to clean themselves, because they would have known, would have sensed, in the isolation of their own creation, that there is a hand, a mouth, a breath, selecting, and if they realized that the birth of a species in which the pain of the mother and the pain of the foetus complete each other, increase each other, dissolve in each other, the pale image of memory and the agony of creation, then perhaps we might recall the instant of birth, which is united with all this pain in an essential boiling, and perhaps we would be able, given the influence of the demonstration of our transitoriness we are not immediately obliged to face the obverse of our birth, we do not perceive time to be a stream flowing away, and in the organization of this world we recognize the power of God, who does not exist in time, nor is he independent of it, but is himself a droplet falling into the waters of eternal truth. Into these waters a falling droplet is of the same matter as the ocean of eternal truth, a wave that cannot split itself asunder, concentric circles endlessly returning into themselves, distinct from and yet indistinguishable from the peaceful still waters of the lake in its basin, like the circular mirror of the well that is as deep as the soul, and if doubt runs through us, then perhaps we are able to believe with joy that the wind races in the night, through rocky barren hilltops and stony forests, with needle-leaved pine trees, cypresses, and beneath the earth's tortuous suffering, with its ripped crust, at the sole point of our world, in that cave, then used as a stable, on soiled straw, among the animals and the shepherds, like a momentary, floating star, when timelessness does not take the step into time, nor does time itself spin dizzily into eternal truth, but at the interstice of time and timelessness, the sound made by a child at its first sharp intake of breath, he who was born but not created of the Father, and he had dominion over everything.

Only the flashes of God's light enter our mind, as if far in the distance his lighthouse beam spread light across the sea. We do not know whether it is star or city sparkling on the water, a light that does not reach us from the sky through the medium of the air and does not reflect back, prompting rays of light from the glass-hard and shivering mirror surface of the waters, but from an unknown source, perhaps originating in the depths of our own eyes. There are bright dancing points of light on the velvet veil of the darkness, innnumerable and existing in incalculable instants of time. Tiny points of light are extinguished with the shivering of the waves in the actuality of this light-dampening matter. God is not only ungraspable but unimaginable as well and through every manifestation that we may perceive the least in the finality of timeless existence we finally name as destiny. We are finally able to live through that which is finally named as destiny, in its perfection of the experience of imperfection, above which every conscious infinity is able to contemplate a finite form, as if identical with itself and alienated from that which runs in parallel with itself. And thus we conceive of our own helplessness and our veiled suspicions draining through light in its own illusoriness. Our heart breaks off and falls downwards into pain which can approach eternal truth as if for one single instant, and only for one single instant, it had stepped into finite time. For there was a greater step that this, and therefore a more terrifying and inconceivable step than creation itself, which did not transform his existence but did transform his being, him for whom existence and essence are indistinguishable. After that strength was undermined, the strength that contains in itself all things, our heart tears in an attempt on the strength of God, infinity stirs into shuddering motion, leading into finiteness. In this form of finiteness lies the transitoriness of man, not simply that inner shudder, by which we sense within us our fear at its sacred inexorability, but that it is itself a sacred and immeasurable suffering, a transitoriness more complete than any other, and therefore our life does not take a transitory form, in the span of life of a human being the world's all becomes immeasurably small, by our human ability to conceptualize, with thirty-three years expressible in an instant that was both itself and abandoned by itself. He who does not believe, because he is himself belief, not only the one in whom they believe, but the very outflowing of the essential possibility of belief, like light reflected, inhabiting the human soul, faith an event and faith an object of dedication, more complete and more perfect than human faith, which contains within itself – even at the same time as he who believes, within his human concepts the entering of hells of doubt and uncertainty – the self abandoned by the self, the division of God, who seeks to know himself and to take on human form, not only distanced from himself as from myself, but from God as from unnameable secrets at an infinite distance, truly God alone, he who – and this is not just one single essence of godliness – is both himself the God and the unknowable God himself, and if we were to say ourselves, with this I and you cannot in his world be excluded from godliness, but as existing beings enter the condition of deepening into the self, the self that is the contemplation of everything. At the same time we know that a picture of the self cannot reflect from nothing, from that which mirrors itself alone, the non-existent shell that surrounds the borderless border of all things, the virtual spherical coating reaching only the inner border of the world, its concentric surface. God's human contraction appeared at one instant in time, in the infinity of the saints. Fissures appear in this veil of light, cracks that peel away and allow the process of the evaporation of death to flow into creation, the nothingness in relation to which creation stands in opposition. (May God be identified with existence, even an alienation, or originate from the other, the fabric of the created world, as after creation can nothingness exist?) This eternally shrivelled mortal is able to conceive every break in the shell of perfection so that that which is torn and that which is entire is in time incapable of selection and indistinguishable. When God with the power of a word created the world, and then not that word itself but the word made flesh became a part of the created world.

And that godlike knowledge, from which we imagine he does not perceive the fragmented vision of division, the ability that appears at the same time both a blessing and a curse, but still at one time a blessing like a gift, and in such a human characteristic we do not perceive any interdependence with the sacred – although is it possible for there to be something in man that does not depend on God? – the ability and compulsion to break into pieces, which we in our everyday world substitute for godlike vision, but which in actuality is immeasurably the less, truly in the eyes of God the perfection of the unfragmented image, with colour shadings infinitely richer than in our vision, and yet so much more complete that one could never realize our way of perceiving fragments as joining together into the one or scattering into the many, perhaps this godlike understanding can survive its own strange suffering, the borders around it sealed and the perception of suffering fragmented, the knowledge of the being who lives again and again, and through this living again and again knows not only himself and the finiteness of the world but recognizes finiteness as the ancient origin of misery, recognizes borders as an instrument for enclosing us, the animal pen that defines the space of our life, the holes through which the river of our existence runs away, and that the finiteness, the enclosure, the pressure through which we ascend, for only by this and for this are we able to rise above the holes and towards ever unreachable freedom until we can guess, as freedom is simply the sensation of difference without borders, and for God that it is possible within a space utterly filled with matter to create a space utterly filled with some other matter, and that these two, different the one from the other, in precisely the same location in precisely the same instant fulfilling every consequence of existence, and with this the gate in front of us was opened, the fissure in the canopy of the sky through which the sense of different orders of existence can flood into the captivity described by the finite borders of our life, in this prison, with its grilles and bars and stale air, which mistakenly circulates through these cages, in these ever narrowing walls, endlessly reflect back our instants, arrows reversing their trajectories, again and again penetrating our eyeballs, the bleeding wound like a chasm in our membranes of sight, and perhaps for this reason, for the wall from which the arrows rebound is at the same time a wall of darkness, sapping the arrows of their momentum, and yet it is of such a light that it blinds whoever is drawn into the ambit of its illusory brilliance, because it sears the eyeball, first to a scarlet glow and thence only to cinders and ash and the grey bowl of the hollow once filled with nerve endings. So in creation God loves only with the majesty of God, awakening a being to life, protected by love, dying from terror at this majesty. In the realization of this duality we perceive another kind of daybreak which is itself life: a hairfine bridge, a knife-edge path across a hilltop, between a steep stone wall and a bottomless fissure, the boulder of the existence of God broken and dropped into nothingness. In the slow settling of the fragments of earth is conceived the seed that then breaks the crust and gives birth to light, existence transfigured with its own anguish, more elemental than any other sensation, relating to existence as God's existence itself relates to human life, the way creation relates to birth, destined from eternity for this new event, death, which God took on himself, on our behalf, and our passing *into time, when the guardians of the house tremble and the strong men take the burden and the mill girls stop working and the view beyond the window grows dark. Locked outside the doors, as the humming of the mill grows quiet, they awake at the sound of a bird, and the singing maidens become more gentle . . . On the road in all directions they are afraid. The almond tree blooms, the locust drags itself along and the dill bursts because a man is going to his eternal home, and the mourners fill the streets. For before the breaking of the silver rope and the smashing of the golden flagon the bucket is torn from the spring and the wheel of the well is broken. Dust becomes earth once more and the soul returns to God, who gave it.*

The soul of God cannot return to God himself because it was not God who granted it. God did not create the soul of God and if he returns to his source and origin it is not to the creating of God but to God himself that he returns, in the agony of his own death, given for himself, because it is through God himself in his physical embodiment that we witness the eternal creation of singularity and duality, we ourselves, for whom creation of the one and of the two bears witness to the unbearableness of our life and the sanctity of our existence, for us this is simply the possibility of a fissure in our enclosed world, a secret door into an infinity of unknown worlds opening before us, if then we perceived one, now that one will be two, and each, and fragments of both, can change into an infinite multitude, because the two are not from two entire units standing beside each other, but from two complete divisions emerging from one single unique entirety. And he who was born, not created, of one essence with the father and although at his birth God and man were divided, until that instant (and after that instant also) indivisible (because both boundless and endless), and only God remained, for all eternity an inviolate and inviolable entirety, with the human torture of birth and death, the eternally singular being in its duality, ungraspably raised to the godhead and ungraspably individualized into humanity, the agony, with which and only with which the duality is dashed against the solidity of the created world, now become rock, boulders of stone, like sculpted pain solidified, as the mother mourns her children, that eternal emblem of the torment of childbearing and birth, and like that other emblem tearing free and pulling back, that of the loyal disciple who against his loyalty – or perhaps because of his loyalty? – denied his master three times, and so forcefully three times, before the cock crowed twice, because God the creator spoke words and numbers and with the actuality of these formed the world, formed it with words and shaped it into a solid structure with numbers, although in actuality these numbers are ungraspable and are not identical with those by which we define our human measurements. Perhaps by the laws of existence indefinability seeps through our skin, like poison gas, swirling out of the broken ampoule, permeating our body to the marrow of our bone, dissolving the tension of our existence and the tension of sensation in our veins, the abandonment, the suffering engendered by the fear of death, the spiralling indeterminacy in the blood and the marrow, because the essence of our suffering is that we are compressed by finite and measurable distances, as between the sides of a triangle, yet these measurements are inexpressible through human conceptualization, the lengths of the perpendicular sides of the triangle do not conform to our system of numbers, and this straight line, defined by the co-ordinates of these two end points (our birth and our death) skews into another angle into the actuality of another medium, incapable of perception by us, away from the dominion of earthly measure. Can the qualities of matter – length, weight, density – be recorded? If this is not the case and if only a single measurement of non-measure is measurable, it would lose its value. The actuality of matter is not identical with actuality, which is only one aspect of matter and not its essence. Thus, for the body, the sensation of suffering is not the same as some measurement taken from outside the body, something not starting within the body, but taken into the body and within our body not diminishing pain. The essence of Christ's earthly journey is not simply that he experienced human suffering to a divine degree but that human suffering was raised to the level of divinity and because of what remains here on earth of that suffering is consecrated, like the fallen dust of holiness, still touching, glittering on the surface of things as a pollen of no physical actuality, ready for the inhalation of the soul into soulless essence. Holiness without suffering can enter the world, appear within it as a man, move the world divided from God into suffering, because human birth means God separating himself from his godliness, entrusting himself to be the Son of Man, gambling his godhead and because of this instant awaking of the world into a true existence without God. In that instant, when the tortured words of *Eli, Eli, lama sabachthani* rang out and with a great cry he sent out his soul and this cry enabled God, in his experience of nothingness, waking to the knowledge of his own resurrection, in the nauseous absence of his own self, the four corners of the earth trembling, the rending of the temple veil, the graves letting forth their dead, because it was not the Son of Man who died upon the cross, but he who is immortal and eternal (blessed be his name) and in that instant too we who were born into this world, the membranes of our cells, the tissue of our bones, might enable us to experience this earth as a physical body; we guard the image of that terrible fall, the ancestor image we carry, the source of all our subsequent suffering, the swirling as matter takes on solid form, taking into itself and into its atoms the nothingness built into the grilles and cages between creation and birth.

But he who was not created cannot know death. The miracle on which our existence is founded, the transformation of God, giving birth and being born, through the mutual suffering of mother and child, appearing among us in the actuality of his body, a man, he who was never mortal and yet in his godhead sweated the blood of mortality, who took on himself the events of birth and death, thus stepping into a continuum of time and sanctifying it, not only because wherever he trod radiates for ever, that the flowering fields of Galilee are still filled with dazzling brightness, that the surface of the waters of Cinneroth still describe a wake from the position of his boat and his step, and that a godlike destruction, perhaps as punishment for sin, did not bring to an end this windswept land, which, on entering it, we sense as the navel of the world, as if we might climb a rope ladder up out of this rocky landscape into the radiant blueness above, not only because he took on himself human form on earth like the imagined gods of Greek mythology, addressing us directly, but eating our bread, drinking from our cup, his heart radiating human love and suffering the barbs of solitude, but that through him man might be distanced from God as God was distanced from himself, because this transformation, in which this God journeyed to the end of distance and became remote from himself, immersed as another entity in the created world, there on the wooden cross for in the instant of death and for all eternity on our behalf, bursting into flame from this incomprehensible unity, two extreme poles of existence, two different universes intermingling and the ignition releasing nuclear energy, not on a flood of suffering, and not through suffering, which does not disappear with redemption but is sanctified, because God becoming man is not the event of his being born and not the event of his dying, but simply that suffering, the fear of being distanced from God, which he and all of us up to that instant in time experienced as fear of death, and which he experienced more deeply and with more pain, for he was close to the one from whom he feared abandonment and in that separation he was separated from himself. The world and God himself killed for ever the sundered body: the man dragging the cross to the end through the streets of the town, people coming and going beside him and paying him no attention, those whom as a man he had come to love, buckling under the weight, those who stripped him naked and whipped him like an animal, those who pressed a crown of thorns on to his brow and together showed him less mercy than they would a murderer, climbing up the hill towards his own agonizing death, not a liberation from bodily agony, nor from spiritual agony, which in pain became one with the body, because he, whom until this instant his disciples had not believed would not stand under direct peril of death, saw his own body alight with holy fire, human isolation springing again and again from what they were obliged to experience, the flames within his eyes invisible, at that final supper when he saw the sacrificial lamb as a holy being, and as a human being recognized the symbol and the actuality of that destiny he had taken on himself as a sacred task, metamorphosing his own godliness into the fruits of the earth, changing it into bread and wine, and thus sanctifying the created world, removing all from his body that was not created. And this body lost its godhead. And death now, not of himself but through God weighed on him, at the stations of the cross struggling with ever more intense suffering, his steps ever more racked with pain, finally on the highway of human history, the knowledge of the godhead radiating ever further outwards from him. There would have been no suffering if there had survived one shard of hope within him, if he had believed in another essence, in the godhead, but now the sky and the land grew black in front of his eyes, because in his abandonment by God he suffered deeper despair than was possible for any other being. For us it is always granted that we should have hope in the grace with which we are received by God, but he, racked on his own body, died within his godhead, and knowing that the death of God means the implosion of the world, the crumbling into the chasm, the falling into nothingness. He knew that his human death as his godly death fell into the void of nothingness, or shall we say into the void of absolute hopelessness or the isolation of being sealed off from everything. The star of our redemption shimmers on the mirror surface of the well of our non-redemption.

If there is one who addresses, who in the eternity of creation with this addressing again and again creates man and the roaring and heaving tide of humanity, instant by instant, re-creates my life, does he as I address him transform from he who is addressed into he who addresses? In the uncertainty of my hesitant existence how could I differentiate the desire for my addressing to be an answer from the desire that his addressing drains out of me, the desire to address him? I wish that the silence that greets the shouting of my addressing cry, absorbing all other sound like a wall, would be his silence. Would this silence might spring from a vibration unperceivable to the sensory organs that pick up human words? And would this silence be a circle of his enclosing with concentric circles enclosing each other, as it were closed in on themselves, containing nothing but themselves, these ever radiating circles filling the surface and the depth, radiating out from each other, rippling, extending, stretching out to infinity, the finite infinity of God, the unaddressable circles' pulsing density? Because his suffering was submerged in itself his sacrifice of himself creates for us an ungraspable otherness, for the water the darkness and for the darkness the water. His death does not mean that for us every dying is an abandonment by God, his every suffering a suffering into which we sink: to follow his suffering would submerge us into hopelessness, to share with him the deprivation from himself for three days, between death and resurrection. How could we know if God created the world in order to fill it with the radiation of his suffering or, on the contrary, that suffering is what lifts his image above the waves? Would man have addressed God if he had not been addressed himself, this mute summons that articulates for us the silent word we do hear or allow ourselves to hear? Do we only hope that with that final cry with which he gave up the ghost we also tumble into the soot black of the night of hopelessness, because what can we expect instead: suffering for ourselves, which with its own ecstasy conjures God or the suffering of God by which he takes our suffering into himself? We suspect we were created out of the suffering of God and born out of our own, to journey further away and to arrive closer to that which is still not divided between *the waters which were under the firmament* and *the waters which were above the firmament*. Was the world created for us to die in the birth of God and for us to be resurrected with his death, our only refuge in the blood-sweating suffering of his absence?

BETWEEN

Love and Madness

I did love you once.

Indeed my Lord, you made me believe so.

And then you said, *You should not have believed me.* Between the two, like an arc of light, of life, like birth and death. One unique spark, the spark of creation, which ignites in the light radiating from God and dwindles in the darkness that is the darkness of God. Like the soft velvet sky, despite its metallic resonant cupola, like the blackness of his seas and the sea above the waters, all the waters not yet separated by the taut canopy. This canopy is none other than the silk-fine membrane of *Indeed my Lord, you made me believe so*, the taut consciousness between existence and non-existence, the inner surface of which is known as belief and the outer surface of which is known as resistance, and we do not know whether it floats on the border that separates existence from itself or that separates the two conditions of non-existence. This emblematic spherical shell – which is not a crust, an outer layer, and still less a fissure – cannot be compressed into space and cannot be defined in terms of space, yet it remains as space, dividing spaces from each other. Or maybe not spaces but simply types of matter, different forms of matter which are not even matter. It divides the sea and the canopy of the sky, where I am water, the upwardly yearning, the whispering in the ebb and in the flow, the never still rippling incapable of stasis, and you are the one who covers the holiness and covers me too, you who would have no name and who is also my dwelling place, the place for my cradle and my coffin. Were this to be my home, if with it and by it actuality were possible, if it were not love, if it were not belief, this rippling on a silk-fine membrane, on this canopy, if it were not a play of light and shadow, which from its glittering and its reflections creates the shell . . . This transparent fabric is an illusion, in actuality it is not a fabric, not holding in its egg our dual body, not forming into a body the dual soul. The naming of this illusion tantalizes us: profound belief is simply a game in which the suffering soul creates the body, that which is united with you in joy, rising into the world or sinking down into itself, so that even in forming and re-forming the soul is ungraspable; it is purely itself, with its own homogeneity, which nothing and no one can disturb, which in its unbounded form no one can break into, the formlessly perfect form that no one can tear asunder. Only the soul of God, who is more real than his own homogeneity, able with concentration gradually to pour himself into and enter into substanceless existence, elements of his being into creation, again and again, into flesh, skin, arms, legs, into hair matted together and the ebb tide of engorging and detumescent organs filling each other and touching each other, stroking and slapping, steaming with heat and vapour, transforming into sound, into moaning and gentle sobbing, and after this taking on the guise of invisibility, that we should never know. The *You should not have believed me* is the builder and destroyer of this illusion, and death, voluntary death, there beside the stream, in the garden, among the flowering roses and the rhododendrons, in the house, which, for me, for the hours and for the fleeting days of my life, was my only home, and this your burial chamber, your vault, became for me the ensured place of my past and future death. For you, who instead of a man loved a woman, and for me, who instead of a man loved God, our death, suffering for each other, the redemption of each other, or revulsion into eternal damnation, you and me, Ophelia, still writhing against each other, into death, the *in truth, glory*, and you would not have believed how the illusion of actuality is extended with life-saving rope, the illusion of the truth of those who are not believed.

Always with this, always with God and always with the absence of God, there is simply the veil of another body, through semi-translucent, lace-edged fabric, the clod of earth in the existence of God, a shadow love, in a light more powerful than any darkness projected into the world, the shadow of another soul, the darkness of which bears witness to that other unbearable light, in this negative reality, the swallowing of darkness, love, like the opening bell of the tulip, deep and bright in the blackness holding substanceless substance, a truer radiation than any graspable truth. The radiance of love can permeate objects and yet itself comprises an impermeable crust, gathering together within its shell and so dense that it becomes absorbant, like the red sun at dawn, the bowl of love, the wall of which is not transparent and is not to be touched, returning into itself, circling round and round, its radiation exciting itself, present existence rendered solid, when the soul fills another existence to the brim, and marvels that it does not spill, does not run over, in this light warmly rippling air, the mist of another being, filling everything, because the one who loves cannot distinguish his own soul from the entirety of the world, and so, in his arrogance, disrupts holiness, the intense glow of his emotions already dissolving into a divine fire of creative strength, but he who is lovesick is more humble than anyone else, because divine creation allows its current to flow through him and he neglects himself and neglects his own life and death. The divine fire burns and the stone-scattering surge of creation flows with him but within the lovesick soul fire does not evaporate water and water does not quench fire, because the elements that feed fire and water are more ancient than the elements of the existing world, and date from the period when God created the world out of existence and tore the creator asunder to create the elements, a self-completeness of fire and water, when divided into substances and souls, into souls floating above the waters; from the period when God created the human but had not yet created man and woman, the human in his own image and likeness, still ignorant of the pain of the cross, ignorant of death. Love remembers such a time, when there was neither love nor death, and therefore no yearning, no one yearning to return to the garden, back into a completeness, which can be found today only in a recognition of the anguish of love, which left its imprint on every stone, on the fern, on the plants of the whispering waterside, on the oak crowns of the hilltops, the pain of the dividedness of duality and the yearning for reunion which commands our every breath, for us and for the world, if not a yearning for reunification, for a gathering of all constituent parts, ever smaller and smaller, beyond the boundary that cannot be imagined, into every hollow, God holding the wave within himself, but God is hollow too and in this cavity he holds in his hands the world (as you once held my face in your hands), the world that, because of what he created, should live through suffering, should suffer for that, God not separating by that transformed timelessness into time and filling the completeness of space, because time became more incomplete, for God alone guards the memory of timelessness and the completeness of space. Beside the identity of completeness, the yearning for differentiation, as those in love exist within each other and the condition of the torn-asunderness of joy, joy in living and joy in death, always together, always once and only always, dwindling into the timelessness of love and rising again, again and again dwindling into the transitoriness of reunion, in the pain of every true embrace, a union more perfect, more painful than the recognition that what must be for two must become one, that we can again find God, and the form of living in which life and death become each other, ever unable to return to the completeness of the eternal existence of God, only the one in love knowing this, in the dark of the night, when the just audible rustling of pearls engulfs the whispering of the slowly passing minutes, pearls separated from another soul, trickling like grains of sand through the hourglass of time, crumbling away, and like fish scales, rainbow, mother-of-pearl, filling the moon room, the bed awash with sweat, the air, like the sea, engorged and ebbed with the moon, soaking and spilling from the window in a sure regular rhythm, slowly burying the one, the one adorned with sparkling glass pearls mingling with rainbow tears, alone the one in love, feeling he exhales the flux and reflux of nature, who knows that his emotions are fragments of the breath of God, the light–dark rhythm of nature like the slow crawling of snails in the darkness, with their spiralled perfect homes on their backs, transforming into perfect symbols of the world for us, like the mute fish in the enclosed sea of liquid glass, bearing witness to God's medium being neither air nor water, but the inconceivable all, as with plants with their instincts and desires which are incomprehensible to us, alone he knows, held in the arms of God, daring to know the certainty of God, that the essence of our existence is its hopelessness.

The one in love is not in love with another but with love. He tries to re-create the completeness of the world through the strength of weakness. He disturbs just enough for the world not to damage its moving harmony within himself. He does not grip things but satisfies himself with simply touching them. In his caressing there is more strength than in the machines that move mountains, its touch returning the soul of the dead one to life and lulling it into a Sleeping Beauty briar-rose dream (and into a rosy-cheeked dream), throwing it into the flame and watching over the flame, guarding it as it sleeps in the epicentre of the flame, and so grows out of the rose, out of the fire, from the glowing brushwood, like Ariel, the angel of the air, seeping through the clay wall of the cave of sleep, as if journeying into the depths of the earth, among roots where long since the earth filled in the graves of the dead with vegetation, into the chambers where death is changed into life, so that life always protects it, holding it within itself in its every drop, born not simply of creation but also of death. This is what love taught, even taught death, contained in the flesh of the apple, the apple that was tasted, the spherical apple of love, there, in the garden, beneath the tree of innocence, and among the animals, but because of that attracting an everlasting curse, but that in the sweetness of the apple there is always a cold flavour, that inexplicable otherness that reminds that that fruit, the fruit of love, did not ripen in this world but elsewhere, on another level of existence, that he came to know it, to make it his own, sealed for all eternity because he gave the order, the prohibition, God decreed the prohibition, and the permission beyond the prohibition, that the parallel of its own dividedness should create the anguish of human betrayal, because for God the pain of the separation of creation, and the pain for man too, the helplessness of falling into sin, because creation was organized as partial, but with this God imagined his own self as partial too, knowing what is good and what is evil, and love was what taught him what was good and what was evil and creation and death.

The hideous contradiction of our destiny is that, as close as we come towards God, so the distance between us grows greater and greater. As we may guess from the sweet breeze of the lost garden, the greenish halfshade beneath the trees, through which glinted the golden light of the sun and the silver glow of the moon and a kind of light beyond our imagining, letting us, as through a glass darkly, see the blurred stains of the sun and moon in the sky, and how much stranger for us is this garden, in which nothing has withered and decayed. When, by the strength of love we summoned forth birth from out of the opaque fabric of creation, we summoned forth dying as well. We fulfilled the promise of the Scripture, in our sundering we become again at one with God, through that sin for which man has not been forgiven, that in the state of love he becomes a god. He is filled with the mercy of God, except that it must be remembered that nothing can resemble God. The human soul, woven out of life and out of death, as the world is woven out of the light and the dark, in his love will become at once humbled, devotion to God transforming him into a god, adoring only a simulacrum of God, who is the one with whom he is in love, in whom, concealed within a cloud of his own sin, embodies the torment and radiance of God. Thus, could love be other than a path between devotion and madness?

In every instant of love, there is a fading away of the chain of perceived causation between sin and punishment. In just such a way are time and space reconstructed, not for each other, but as a result of the variation in the transparent shell solidified from the air and the vapour of bodies. This is what separates all things that once fitted together from each other, separates objects from their individual local medium, which is commonly air, but in the same way separates the myriad sea coral from the water, changing colour as they break the surface, their cellular and interior glistening fading, disconnecting their bodies, even then still fitting closely the one into the other, so closely that they almost dissolve each into the other, the invisible glass skin warming around those in love, beginning to tremble, thus engendering a different kind of vibration, which slowly engenders ripples, with at last the whole world flowing into itself, transforming dissolved colours into those of the sea. This changes the forms of the dissolved world from pain into chaos, dripping out of the soul, which, in isolation, separates from the soul of the one in love and, freezing, stands at the centre point of creation, alone in the palm of God. Yet he cannot protect or shield him. He cannot experience the caressing of a hand but only through the caressing of another human hand, his word, shouted or whispered, becomes comprehensible through the medium of a human voice, and as the soul approaches ever closer to the centre point of God's love, so much closer does it approach to utter isolation, experiencing radiance as blindness and the velvet of darkness as sharp, cold, painful light, by which, as it distinguishes objects from each other, solitude is increased. This light illuminates from a single distant and spherical source, anaemically, as there are no colours to mark a differentiation, and so the colours of the world are fading, and the landscape beneath the moon, without colour, changes into that which for God is beneath the sun, because the shimmering of the lonely bleached God, whose own self even in solitude is at the centre of his own radiance, because man is able to absorb God only in the painful intensity of human love, not in the reciprocity of love, but in the ecstasy of love, because the warmth of the body, the heat of the proximate skin and the glances of opal fire melding together. (In actuality the geometric plane of the glance is not blue, nor blue-green, nor even brown like sadness, and does not originate from the eyes but from the sense of sight, and the rainbow membrane of other eyes changes the light of our gaze from blue to grey and from brown to near-black, changes because it sears the sensations that flow from us, and thus with these changes of colour continuously reverberating, there and back, in permanent colour and the transformation of light, they resonate into being new worlds, and the radiating rays radiated outwards remain invisible to all, like the burgundy red, the blue, the green, welling up beneath the milky surface of the opal.) Glances and words, sounds more exquisite than any note on the violin, music that with its silky sweep conjures up the rippling of the air but is also able to make that same air solidify into a static block of ice, into a block of ice through which the slight vibrations of sound cannot penetrate, that world in which only love is able to make perceptible the handprint of God, the world we lose in the blinking of an eye in that instant when our singularity in love extinguishes for us the weakness of the interwoven glances, in the shivering induced by the snuffed-out oil wick, after the extinguishing of all the candle warmth, we shrivel together, the wrinkles of our skin seeming incapable of receiving the warmth of God. And in the act of transformation into nothingness we approach more closely to the diminishing of God for the world and for us, for people, and in that change, with which he proves his love, we on the contrary experience a turning away and a fading away, because God, when he surrendered the completeness of his godliness, opened a fissure in the perfect surface of the globe, that sphere over which the icy breeze of nothingness should stream, reaching into the erstwhile flowering forest of existence.

Therefore the one in love, if he retains himself, not the nest-builder in the world, but experiencing empty space flowing in from beyond existence, the shivering of which is not a physical vibration, not that of the one who freezes and stands in the drenching downpour in his ice-soaked clothes, between the blowing of the snow and the blowing of the wind, not sensing the surface of the single locked door, the curved beams that can be beaten by fists, but then the footsteps are still not sounding from the far side, do not recognize this house, from the inside of which there is no approaching with a blanket over his arm, one who stands up, dries the other off a little, has him lie down in front of the fire, cradles him in his arms, and the garden, which was once seen in bloom, has now become mud, mire, icy hollows and the attendant retinue of rusting memories. No, left to himself the one in love sees a multitude of doors, the one behind the other, or rather beyond this point one beside the other, and every single one of these doors is shut, in houses that for instants or for days were perhaps a home to him, never to ring again with anticipated footsteps. They mock the gardens, there are bloodstains and dirt apparent, there where once they buried young soldiers, among the flowers and the grass, mixed with weeds, others now go by on the rough soil, others who can never know that here one dawn there bloomed the invisible rose of happiness. The one in love, whom they left behind, stands incomprehending in this world that exiled him from itself, but not him alone, not only he who stands alienated from everything, like an alien being insulated within endless and harmonious creation. No, the world fragmented around the one in love, the structures collapsing into each other, not tumbling in parallel because some strange magnet pulls at them, its poles randomly displaced, the whole world separating its powerful, irregular, circling powers, for which there are still not physical laws for anything that fragments into curving chaotic spirals, in contrast to those that in their contours protect the orderliness of the created world, which according our ancient experience and the dreams and illusion formed of that which we perceive as beautiful. On the other hand there is the handprint of God, the only enduring evidence of creation, by contrast with which all that spirals within us will be hideous, the createdness of the world crumbling together, shapes tumbling into impossibility, with us believing that he who created the world observed the laws of form, separating the upper canopy and the lower canopy, the day from the night, and formed animals of every order and rank so they might populate the world. The world becomes fragments of ugliness if we do not know how to forgive the beauty of God, because by means of this very beauty we feel when we are within it that we are alone, now experiencing nothing but this solitude, only ourself, alone in the turning wind of entirety, and there is no God who would embrace, if not within the embracing arms of the one in love, mistakenly opening, blooming, falling from the flowering crown of the fruit trees. If there is not that sole pair of eyes that we imagine would see within us at a glance; this strength connects together the eyes not deepening into each other, so that each retains the imprint of the other, conjuring spring out of winter, because without this other pair of eyes it is still winter, even if the trees put forth buds and the crowning yellow glory of forsythia bursts beneath your window, what power would be capable, with a murmur of your bitterness below the ground, of bringing back the actuality of winter, with snow covering the petals of the flowering fruit trees and bending low the weak petals of the tulip, what power can it be that does not flow from God and does not flow towards God and inexorably so that, like creation, it gives life and takes life away, merely through existing in the form of the existence of another being? Is it a miracle that if you do not understand this power and you cannot locate it in the crystalline structure of creation, because it is unlocatable in the discipline of above and below, and between the briar roses of separation and union, because it is inexplicable that it should be missing, what is not, and now that which is nowhere in the world: that truly is the love that circulates in your veins as if it is a corrosive substance, fresh with every beat of the heart, spreading ever more burning pain throughout your system, reaching into your limbs, so that now even your skin hurts as if the circulation of the air wounded you and it is sheer agony to have it flow in and out of your lungs. This phantom love, this love of the other – was it never? was it ever? is it gone? – in which you believed has by this instant become unbelievable. Now you do not know whether it was God you worshipped or an idol, or if God himself if he turned his beneficence away from you, the beneficence for which you were so grateful, for by this instant you no longer know how to believe in him whom you loved. Is it miraculous that you experienced the overthrowing of actuality, as if strange forces govern our life, for does it not take an even greater certainty, existence with its victorious continuity, to believe that God-created demons watch over you, from out of shadowy corners and from the shadows under furniture, that the glass in the window is thin, it is almost as if those powers that keep their rays confined lived within its surface, giving into your hand a garland of flowers, and with the sound of an erstwhile audible wind harp luring one to the willow tree of childhood, to the slender dipping branches of the willow, where the end of the gardens becomes the bank of a stream, mirroring the grey foliage, for what you now seek in the flowing water is but the mirror image of the world. Now you seek neither him who is no longer nor the clouds of the sky which now take the place of his face once framed in yours and your face once framed in his, but the incomprehensible draws you to submerge yourself into the vortex of God. How could God permit this? It is your own madness in the whispering of the stream, in his lost voice resonating, that draws you away from the twisted actuality into our twisted suffering.

In this madness absence and presence dissolve indistinguishably together, guarding at one time the duality of their togetherness and of their separation. The souls of those in love interpenetrate each other but in the meantime stand at interstellar distances from each other, not only when the one loves and the other flees or when the one suffers and in the other there is no pity encouraging a hastening to rescue, but if they sit beside each other, in the trance of love, as life continues around them, the peace of a village square possible around them, the present the past simultaneously, for the one the present and for the other a memory, even for one the past, doubly so in the pain of the suffering of the present memory and old space flowing from the soul of the other, the past into which they were allowed, as if they were permitted to walk a little in a strange garden – for whom? for the other? – in their erstwhile home. Who can know this home truly already lives within him, that he created it, the real past memory expelled from him, enfolding his loved one, the space in which they now sit and which holds within him this island, this city, and the sea pounding around the city, becoming the two of them and remaining for ever, the last earthly language of their happiness, with the road floating under their step, which, who knows, may be the same as the road that passes along by the canal. Does it pass there now in the autumn rain, in the dark, used only by workers on their way back home, clerks and gaolers heading for Venice's women's prison, nuns serving God within the communities of prostitutes? Or doctors and mothers hurrying to the children's hospital, mothers suckling their sick children, tears of anxiety, bad conscience or resistance running down their faces. Mothers, among whom I too belonged on this still summery morning, when I could have become your mother, so you could forgive yourself for the sins committed against me, and you could feel my forgiveness, from even beyond the grave. From such a distance you could see me even in the rising smoke from the chimneys of Auschwitz, could imagine me there, and later send yourself there among the dead, to achieve a union with me, again and again testing my forgiveness. Or was it rather that I sought again and again to die, selflessly, to make you experience my love even beyond my own death? Selfishly too, for in the meantime I would be free of the threat of earthly suffering, that in actuality and even with me you would have committed the same transgression, and that only in this transgression would we become the same. Truly you abandoned him, but he did not abandon you, not even when they took him to die. Could he have thought of the other, in that endless moment when the blue-petalled roses of the gas bloomed and their perfume spread, the perfume of the icy terror of death arising from the sweating bodies, under the heavy vapour of the agony of helplessness, an unimaginably chilling current that distinguishes the faith of the dead mingled with their dread, when around the deathbed is anxiety, compassion, adoration, the pulsing waves of – in a word – love. It is not that they take the hand of the one who is stepping into the boat, hesitating for an instant between the bank and the moving boat, hesitating to go into nothingness and fearing nothingness far more than death. There is no need, although caressing is good, the warmth of another body, the closing of the ring of air around our life. There is a need for this, that we should not feel that which we are, our duality, your mother and I, in whom the fear of your mother and your child, the betrayal, unite you with the pain of grief, the horror of abandonment, the terrifying band, stronger than iron, that it is impossible to break even in the spasms of suffocation, which brings our death, wherever it may be, in bed, in hospital, in the green meadow of God or even in the night of some cluttered store room, tracing wisps of cloud in the air, swirling the madness of their vapour above us. What we may not think of you, because more dreadful than this death is that your face is turned away as God turned his face away from his wretched creation, as you try to escape the sight of suffering, only there, where we are now, we now know and see, and even less than how to avoid our own death, we know that your escape leads into the trap of our own death.

Love, a whirlpool, spins into that depth where matter turns and twists within itself, with the mystery of its movement and the deception of sensation of a different density, thus demonstrating its real essence, that by just this much less it differs from most of the substance of the earth than, like deep-drawn water, funnel shaped, or the foaming cataracts and thus in its real essence cannot be denser than those things and still it seems that the essence of the world, which holds itself as if within a single drop and seals in its liquidity. Without it what warms the frozen world, the eternal winter, and we do not know whether it is because of the weighted cold of the snow or the fog or the iron chain stirring inside our bones or whether it is our isolation that freezes the world around us, whether the cold has its origins from the decelerated helplessness of matter or perhaps the converse, the divine power drives variations of temperature into matter, that God directs them to the rhythm of his own heartbeat, to the pulse of divine love, which exists at the point of connection between God and the world, in that instant of timelessness that extended into eternity, and where he disrupts it once more, in the endlessness of a different kind of timelessness, where the radiance of completeness fades the pale stains of desire and hope and in another solitude bleaches things into colourlessness. As hopelessness is incapable of mirroring the sun of God, it absorbs the rays of light into itself and absorbs the world into the half-light of dawn, when there are no shadows and it seems as if there is no reality either, when the empire of the living and the empire of the dead dissolve indistinguishably into each other, because it is in the flame of life that God and the world meet, in carbon and oxygen, and so can we not give the name of love to every flame for this is the essence of love, its interconnection with combustion, as two elements mutually consume the one the other but in such a way that from this elimination of existences springs a further type of matter, a force without physical matter. Is abandonment not a mirrored corridor down which we wander, the one beside the other and also the one within the other, we who see nothing but our own desire reflected in the dull flaking mirrors and not the one who looks through us and returns back through us, he who completes our existence, and beyond that God, whose lightning glare we do not recognize and who cannot move within us except in the form of another human being and therefore compressed his being and his death struggle into a speaking person, so that he would be able to put us to the deepest suffering with him, that we would die with him, that we would die within him, within his pain as we die within him (and therefore can die within him) in the death struggle of our loved one, and the one who endures is no other than the living dead, embossed with eyes and with wax-filled ears, wandering in an earthly swamp, abandoned by God, in a sunless light, for here the sun never shines and never even sets. With no night and no day we wander in the wilderness, although we walk on water, because God has not divided the dry land and the waters, nor has he raised a firmament between the earthly and the heavenly waters. He does not conceive of trees bearing fruit, each named after its own kind, nor of animals, nor of the fish within the water, nor of the fowl of the air (somehow joy sprang in their hearts), nor man, who, created after the image and likeness of God turned back creation and slowly dragged this God-given creation outside the space of the world. He who gave it took it back, the firmament from between the higher and the lower waters; he took back the illuminating heavenly bodies, the plants of the dry land with their fertile branches; he took back the fish swimming in the sea, the birds flying in the sky, the animals with their bellies sliding in the dust and their nimble legs leaping and balancing; he took back the consolation of people and our joy that he created us in his own form, after his own image and likeness, their joy in creation now only the wonder that from the union of two bodies a third comes into existence, the repetition of creation created anew, and that man, created after his own image and likeness, took part in the unbroken chain of creation, yet sealed within us, in our orphanhood and solitude, within us, living through that death, everything the knowledge of which is ungraspable, existence without God, the consolation of which can never glitter in inner resurrection.

Loved ones are transitory; one leaves before the other, and then the other overtakes the first. Sometimes one will look back and wait for the other, each at the edge of the well, either because the one ahead is resting or because the one who follows should offer fresh water lifted up in the hollow of his palms, and drop diamond restoring drops on to the face of the other and stop because of this, because one feels mercy towards the other, who, deathly pale, crawls along in the dust, in order not to leave footprints, or on a street corner where one can vanish from the sight of the other and whoever makes the better progress does not want the other to stop in hesitation and despair without leaving some mark, does not want, not then, for one to choose rather the road of solitary existence, feels real regret that such a profoundly black veil of emotion has enveloped the other, and so does not leave the other to grow numb in the icy night. It is even possible that one waits in the cemetery beside the coffin made of unfinished wood full of splinters, into which after this he will bury the one to come, but he knows he carries the one into the grave happily if, in the final moment, from his point of view, he glides into nothingness. They are transitory but love is not transitory, the imprint of feet that continue to make the earth tremble, shimmering like hot air above the road, transformed into unforgettable memory, the spirit into humus, every soul being born into eternity, forming an abscess on the surface of the world as an ever denser coating, this fog seeming to engulf distant stars in a tissue of light. Love is not transitory, love that nourishes the water of the wells and sets the corner stones, pointing the way to the next open gates, guarding the flowers of the cemetery above the long since sunken graves, because the one who loves is alone, if he has buried his companion, and then also alone, if on the pathway he does not approach the steps of the other, yet if he knows that among the numberless diagonals and curves of the world one is always approaching the steps of another, so powerful is the force that extends with the earth's own magnetic field, intersecting the convexity of the world, and though more constant than any other power of attraction, more constant that the path of the sun and of the moon, than the variations in high tide and in low tide, there is still the utter isolation of perpetual exile into the world and he must experience that loneliness that was never experienced by the one who, in the absence of his only being, never experienced the absence of God, nor his abandonment on the earth, when God turned away his gaze. But love never knows isolation because for love one never exists and two never exists either, but love knows nothing but completeness and its obverse, nothingness. In its completeness turning time gathers together and sinks into mutuality, the soul swells into flame and flares into fire, the sky and the earth, God and his created world unite and dissolve everything into itself, which had previously existed in fragments. In entirety there is no fragment and no totality, no I and no you, or perhaps I could say that there is no definable connection between the essence of fragment and the essence of entirety, and their desires for each other and their unifying with each other remain mysterious. There is only the unending vibration the one within the other of the I and the you, just as the paths of the particles of the atom oscillate back and forth between non-existent planes, or existence and non-reality, or reality and non-existence in circles described by God. Because in the translucent light of God existence and reality are perceived through each other, in the phosphorescence of the substanceless of being, from an invisible undiminishable reality is created the shadow of a lost reality, as if a gauze-like fabric separated from the mist of the water, out of the non-existing rise slowly the curved outlines of the existing, although in the faith of love, when there is no need for the presence of the other, and perhaps even no need of their existence. Our soul would divide into reality and non-existence, existence and non-reality, in such a way that they are able to fill the soul, that out of this space should form, should solidify, the small-town houses, the crumbling church, the home of God, there on the right, long abandoned by people, from the ruins of which, here and there, grass grows, and a scrawny tree tries to cling to the crumbling stony soil, and behind our backs, there is a bridge arching over the canal drumming with the sound of boys and girls racing across in fancy dress, dressed in the outfits of their choice, disguising the insanity of their passion which glows through their skin. The ones who love suffer because everything wounds them, the air enters and leaves their lungs like thorns, like long, spiny claws. If we were to appoach it, the thorns of Christ encircle our garden. The dusk of daylight bleaches the house walls white, and who knows which hurts the more, the slow decay of the trees or that they must bring forth new shoots every year? There is one who has long since crumbled to dust, one who cared for them as children, because the one who loves does not forget, and experiences absence at the time when he meets the loved one's skin with every pore of his own like a unique wound. The hugging is more frequent, the greater the distance over which the two swimmers approach each other and it is never possible to ascertain whether the eddies and currents are not tumbling them further away from each other, so that they shall never meet again, carrying them away into the infinity of the ocean to be despatched in desire, in absence, in the isolation of helplessness. It does not damage love, but it nourishes suffering, which leans on it like a bird with wings outstretched leans on currents in the air, and feeds on it, like a fire consuming itself, the burning bush that never rests, in which the invisibility of God flares into red flame, metamorphoses into eternal tongues of flame. The lovers speak to each other, naming the world and the things of the world, but in the quietness of love stirs the quietness of God, like the barely audible resonance in the air of muffled bells, like the telling of the seasons in the language of the mute, in time, because the lovers are dying, their passions are dwindling into self-consuming incandescence, yet love is everlasting, because the lovers feel such desire for each other, are enclosed within each other and separated from each other, as if they desire union with God, but love is the desire for God and in our human body, separated from itself for eternity, again and again the world relives its suffering.

If you are – and only then – the world changed into reality, and if you are – and only then – the reality of the world, that would mean that the world is beautiful, because *God saw that it was good,* and then the fresh green leaves, no sooner than they hang freely upon the tree, where there are one or two flowers beginning to unfold, ripening is still only a promise of future harvest. The leaves change into a strange material, the diaphanous quality of light combines with a tangible silkiness, and the living boxwood trees build an impregnable wall, although between the twigs and leaves it may indeed be penetrated. The wall is its own border, dividing its own two sides the one from the other. Yet what purpose is served by this separation, except to divide the air in two, because it is always inseparable, from the inside and the outside of every border and every enclosure it is the same, and so we can do no other but perceive the boxwood wall as a miracle, for if we journey into the depths of seeing, where the two types of separated matter unify, dividing the rigidity of lace and uniting it in the incandescence of its inner transformation so that this miracle of separation and unification becomes itself an emblem of life, no longer a wall, but still that which, bordering itself, a hedge bound by its own inner cage, and if we gaze for long enough, in this windless statis, it is as if we may see the changing colours of the tiny rigid leaves. It is not simply the passage of the sun and the shivering of the breeze causing the fluttering shadows over the evenly clipped plane, but the energy of growth, the transforming power of the earth, into air, into beauty, into the illusion of the visible, which takes on the appearance – and always only the appearance – of matter. We must watch the world for a long time so that all that which is the essence of our world we perceive only in the appearance of a single form, which we must love many times, and which many times must disappoint us, so that we may name this reality if it is he whom we love – and only then – and perceive the illusion of the world, and absorb the ordering of God, who locates manifestation before us in the form of beauty and reality and thus makes it possible for us to accept the singleness of being and reality concealed each within the other, with the jeopardy that this ever self-revealing face of God (the disappearance of being into reality and the invisibility of reality in being) should guide our steps to the gate of near-madness. But it is also within this jeopardy to be halted at this grim and frightening gateway. If God engineered the miracle of creation, then a part of this miracle was to make us able to endure this miracle. And he engineered a greater miracle still, sealed into its miraculousness like a jewel or a piece of amber; he made us capable of seeing in one single drop of his world, through the ungraspable medium of a single pair of eyes, the radiance of his creative power. If all these miracles had occurred, then we would believe too that he compressed himself not simply into something personal but into a person, if we are able to free ourselves from the indescribable crushing fear of the sacred, if we feel the touch of God in the embrace of our lover and to sense a form of prayer, turning towards God, in our own love. Because in love the one who is in reality a man is transformed. In the vertigo of his existence within us he becomes God's agent, an angel, pure existence. And in the flame of this double ecstasy the ungraspability of existence takes on within him human form, just as the outpouring of the soul of God on earth was disguised by human form.

How could it be impossible for the love of God that our human heart should assume desire for a love taking form in human touch and recognize this creation as the lover first longs for the assumption of the love of God, wishes to be a utensil in which the droplets of the light of creation may be held, but can it then be forgiven that incessantly through this and through man streams an enticing illusion, which leads as much to death as it conjures life and so places the majesty of God before us, concealing that constantly human face, with its definition filled like the face of God and emptied like the face of God, concealed by the ebb and flow of happiness and suffering that we know as passion, and which tangles our sense of sight, ever luring us further into the maze of the nightmare-fired, spark-lit labyrinth. Having us believe we can find our way back to the garden where the same purple and yellow pansies look the same to us as those of our childhood, asking and answering with their glancing hearts and eyes, and again we hear the susurrus of the willow branches answering our unspoken questions in the mysterious shadows of our erstwhile daydreams. This slightly green, yellow, drooping willow has already become grey, and perhaps it does not even exist, or only as its own mirror image in the brook. This brook deceives the face that leans over the water. In this mirror image there is another pair of eyes, the gaze of a fairy luring her into the deep, because this girl could not endure the icy nightmare flame of the dark. She could not bear the love that is there even when it does not exist and exists even if there is nothing.

Indeed my Lord, you made me believe so – and by now I do not believe, the spell is broken and I, *that suck'd the honey of his music vows*, wait like a beetle in the grass to be trodden on by the incomprehensible, terrifying power that is stronger than anything, not abandonment but the anguish of uncertainty, because *I did not love you* – and we, the onlookers at this tragedy, all who see them after their double deaths, in timeless distant past, and yet lying hand in hand on the sarcophagus of our own future. And we recognize in the dignity of their roles the essence of our undignified destiny. Because by now we know that the measure of love is beyond measure, and there is no evidence that could bring us a sense of safety for

> *forty thousand brothers*
> *Could not (with all their quantity of love)*
> *Make up my sum*

yet still at the graveside, here, in the palace gardens, among the neglected Roman courtyards, with what kind of petals does love, now and ever grieving for the dead, bloom? *There's rosemary, that's for remembrance. Pray love remember.* I ask you, even after my death, if I should live then in *muddy death*, in a watery ditch, at the bottom of the grave, or if I am become a wisp of smoke, a cloud, which was *almost in shape like a camel*, although, *methinks it is like a weazel*. I know that you will not remember me, because this love is a sin, in the way that every passion is, as is that of this maiden too, who mourns a murderer, not consciously breaking away from him, neither in sin nor in death, because in fact this is love, which does not disappear into the blackness of the final moment, in the place of execution of our own abandonment, to sleep with murder in the coffin, because the one who loves better loves his murderer than his own murdered self (or loves the murderer concealed in the labyrinth of the soul, perhaps himself alone?). With affection, which crystallizes out of this love, like crystallized order cooled out of lava, from a waterfall, from the glowing core of a meteor, emerging through the whiteness like one angel grieving for the sin of another, doing penance in his place in the caustic flames and fumes of hell, in the crematorium of his burned bones, as a burning curse for a later sinner, penned into the stone enclosure of the as yet not committed, away from those who slumber in their heart, ever unliberated, within the heart of one who will commit a crime, even in the heart of the one who commissions that crime – and whose is the greater sin? – the one who commits (action has three elements, as follows: causing the event, executing the event and committing the event), or the one who awaits the secret handing over, who enforces the committing of the act, with his underground powers, still more so if the blade of the murdering dagger is a single all-encompassing sentence: *I did not love you.* The unavoidable and unbearable destiny is that for the sake of them both and more painful than for the one who stabs, than for the one who is stabbed, because the pain of joining and separating is stronger than the joint existence of duality, where there is no solitude and still the lonely life grows overwhelming, into a powerful shadow moving on the wall behind us, and even then, if the hero approaches closer to his future love, in the helplessness of his destiny, if there is a repetition of every ancient image of love, the love of parents, the son with his mother, the words of the dead father whispered repeatedly into the terrified ear, jealously for the guardian of love and jealously for the father, because love is a hideous labyrinth where lovers are their own paths, as they wander hesitantly, one following the other and one within the other, and who is to know whether we love with a nurturing love of murder the usurper of our love, or the dead one who rises in his spirit form, transforms and appears, invisibly, in the room, in the bed, in the heart, which does not see but into visibility for the sake of the boy who, if he loves his mother, is in love with his mother and is in love with love of his mother, torturing himself with love, a torture in which it is not possible to love him who frees us from our greatest rival. It is not possible for us not to hate the one whose deed mirrors our own desire, it is enough in the helplessness, that we do not want to kill him, the one we so much love, that we put ourselves in his place, place ourselves in the desire for this reckless deed, which the sky refused us courage for, able to conquer him, excluded from grieving and deciding, in the wild lunacy of new love, uniting grief and the lust of guilt, depths of mourning and pangs of conscience, where there is no more thought because our existence would be unbearable if we were to look infidelity, sin and our own desire in the eye, if in fact we look ourselves and each other in the eye, but it is disappearing into the body of the other, as if we were pressing a dark velvet cushion on to our face, smothering ourselves in the thoughtless darkness, in the nothingness, into the depth in which love and death are indistinguishable, because both are themselves escaping, fleeing in terror, throats tightening into suffocation, the heart drumming in the ears, in which delayed death oozes in, because in the blood-boltered stage play, signifying life in our times, the mother and the son of our times, its harsh circumstances, and fathers, friend, beloved, and the flowers in the hand of the girl who has lost her mind, who gave herself in all innocence, on St Valentine's Day, at dawn in the house and afterwards did not wander in all innocence between the grave and the path by the stream, not in all innocence because she resisted her love, which she was later compelled to suffer again, and so can we say that it was in all innocence that she died? Love still raised up . . . As it was, the fairy temptress, abandoning and abandoned in the actuality of creepers and ivy, where everyone is in love with everyone else and everyone hates everyone else, because love so penetrates the crust of the earth's globe, eggshell thin, its rim tinkling and chiming like rivulets of water and the air between its solidities, when all were bodies born of love and dying in love, clinging to one another, or falling away from one another, and there we remain, still living and watching this tragedy, briefly in the lightning flashes of destiny tumbling blindly into the crevasse opened by the earthquake, squatting on the floor, our scattered threads spinning and tangling, unknowable and unstoppable in our hands, as we try again to knot together love and madness.

BETWEEN

Fate and Destiny

The bullfight: in the magic spell of its instants, like a very light elastic ball spinning on a water jet, on the pinnacle of its existence, dancing on the eternal presence of the jeopardy of falling. No one knows what holds it there and the column of water itself constantly curves and sways. Leaping only because the water jet again and again describes an arc, the noose going upwards and coming downwards, appearance and disappearance, coming into being and nothingness. In the instant of the ball dancing in the air, which perhaps is not even in the air, not in the dispersed illusion of the edge, but pirouetting in nothingness, it appears as if it is its own motion that keeps it up within nothingness, floating on wings as if it would become something out of nothing after all.

And these instants are the very commencement of a series of instants, when on this already warm and long Sunday afternoon early in summer as the hands of the clock read five to five. There is the imperceptibly slow slipping past of the thick black numerals and still everyone senses this blow as greatly different from any other. Time, which, until now was approaching a goal, a beginning, as much the ending of the waiting until now as the beginning of something utterly other, the opening chord of of an inexpressible narrative, when the master of ceremonies ascends the podium. He raises his baton and the door in the eye-level barrier swings open. Two men, flourishing long feathers in their caps, dressed in solemn black, trot round the arena, stand and bow deeply before the ringside box of the president, who is dressed in civilian clothes. Our eyes are suddenly aware of the contradiction and the difference: high up there is the presiding judge of the fight, like some priest of the gods, wearing a well-cut suit and tie, smiling a lordly smile. Down here is that on which he will pass judgment: victory beyond death. And for one moment the difference between the time in this entertainment and the time of our own present strikes us. This breath-stopping paradox does not exist only out of timelessness and these two passing hours of our peaceful Sunday afternoon. These two hours may be perceived as standing between erst-while traditions and presentday appearances. Something else that is different is visible too: the gold and silver of the quadrille, the pale-flowered brocaded costumes, the elegant colour of the knee-length silk stockings, the fine tripping on lightweight shoes on one side of the arena. The audience sit all around and there are some men who are only half dressed. They sit here as once no one would present himself in public, like those who do manual labour, on the land or in slaughterhouses, those who toss and turn in illness sweating in their sheets, those who exist within the ecstasy of love, and women as well, emphasizing their femininity not with their beauty but with vulgar provocative fashions. We sense the pain of the origin of all this. We sense the pain of that world sinking downwards until this instant, how it came to lose the dignity of the great fights, the drama of life and death. The world in which the observance of the old ceremonial continues now only in two theatres, from Sunday to Sunday. We gather together, to celebrate, as with that other death and sacrifice offered up within the soul, that it lives on in mortal bodies. We are bewitched by the ancient entertainment, when the bullfight starts, and the heart fills to overflowing with excitement. Like a golden cloud above the ring and into the enclosed arena flows the breath of mortality and the heart begins to dance on a rising and falling jet of wild anticipation, in the nothingness, or in the glory of the instant. Because here life becomes a single instant, even narrower than an instant, on which minute fragments of time compress together. If movement and time belong together, only divisions of time notated with irrational numbers can express movement beyond time. This movement, in which we always sense the closedness of time, as we sense condensation on the points of leaves on a tree becoming droplets; from an oval gradually a globe is formed, rolling downwards from certainty to uncertainty. They fall into the puddle and lose their essence; they lose themselves, like the susurrus of pearls cascading from a broken necklace, one after the other. We sense time passing, or still we sense the miracle, the feeling forbidden to me, time as passing, the embracing and parting of *is* and *was*, this archetype and essence of every love, and the instant beyond time when the fallen droplet or the pearl tumbling away exist only as a memory. When it acquires knowledge of an event, it has already occurred; after it has occurred we see it and hear it. It relives within us only in the form of spreading rings; on the passing of its actuality, we sense the illusion of its actuality. With a flourishing of caps the knights in their finery and all the members of the quadrille have marched away. The gate opens and, dazzled in the sudden light, the bull runs in. The curtain goes up and in a naked momentary existence theatre and audience face each other, separated by the dividing and impassable wooden fence and united in that experience, which is an imitation and also an archetype of the greater things of the world. In fact the curtain of the soul is raised, but at the same moment it also descends, right round, by the high wall of the arena, and what will now take place in the timeless instants of the ensuing two hours will happen here. Only in the ring and only in the soul, which observes every movement of the conflict, the heaving, the twisting together, the onrush, the bowing and withdrawing configurations. This then, a series of blinding flashes, like arabesques described by lightning, is the devastating ecstasy of the fight.

Two forces drive on and two forces hold back the players.One is the combat with the audience, because the matador spreads his scarlet cloak like a deck of cards and twists the fabric into nothing, a space not visible to us, into the width of a single ray of light entering our eyes. He continues the conjuring show, appearing and disappearing, witch-like transforming the one into the other, the bloody actuality, the lifting up and the crashing down into the dust, the force binding them ever more tightly with the glittering light of illusion. In its reality we freeze this sparkling, this entertainment, the essence of every tragedy. This is what draws our eyes, attracts and holds our gaze on the fluttering *muleta* and thence opens it out on to the whole arena. The curious, excited sparkling of these eyes is for us an invisible element of the spectacle, immersed as we are within what we see and hunting after newer and newer sights, raking the sand backwards and forwards, almost ruffling it. The power of the knife-blade of the material world radiates from these eyes, strafing the ground and then nailing every single fragmentary element. Almost a glint of light of the gaze-sword, a glittering metal plane jumps and curves in the radiance. In these eye-rays there is no compassion, no consideration of another. These instants never extend into infinity, flatly beneath heavy eyelids. In vain I try to recall another kind of glance, a gentle gaze melting into the sky, which from the crown of a hill merges horizontally in the infinity of the eye-coloured twilit heavens.

Here, where the vividness of sunlit colour with its sharply defined lines separates from the blackness of shadow, we do not know which is the more blinding: the light itself or the power of the light to flood the pupils with darkness. Here, in the incomprehensible vortex of this southern city, where these eyes exist within me, daydreaming in the distance, into nothingness, into the past, eyes who seek, through wandering and closing, to dissolve into the past, into nothingness. And what became of my own past, which I longed for so often, like a drop of blue ink mingling into the colourless ocean of forgetting? But this ocean was not washed into colourlessness; rather the seas of complete existence, independent of us, were tinted with the petrol blue of our suffering. Here, in this stage show, as spectators we become like the sons of these southern people who perhaps the more freely (but it cannot be with more commitment than mine) throw themselves into that role, thus themselves taking their part in the drama.

He who is a spectator at this majestic show – how can he even know that although he is completely and absolutely spellbound in the spectacle, it is not the unfolding sequence of the spectacle but the unknown ensuing conflict he sees before him. Not the spectacle itself, but the quickly changing sights, the extraordinarily dense sequence of events, which, because of the depth of the empathy involved, are no longer sights but what we might experience as the surge of events. This unfolds in the ring independently of the actuality of what is occurring. How can he know he is a protagonist in this entertainment, and simply with the movement of his gaze, of his eye-rays (this occurs before the thought reaches his mind), that it is he who directs events? Events burst into flower for him and vanish into nothingness between the other two players, during the time when, in the heat of combat, they are able to pay attention only to each other and cannot even notice us, the spectators, because a momentary absence of concentration would prompt an unavoidable ending. Still this trinity, the two fighting with each other and those committed to their conflict, have no option but this interconnection, because without this rapt involvement, their games of destiny with each other would not be playable. However it would not be indispensable for those who doubly experience to the marrow of their bones their own duality, and their enslavement to the duality of the other.

For a mysterious eternity the world we see differs, in its depth, in its essence, and also in its substance, which is distinct from that which human eyes have never reached. The essence of this fateful game does not exist in order to permit the man in front of us, incessantly, to approach the inescapable, but this vision, which thus far may be followed, exists for the vision that we can scarcely follow, for us, who wait and yearn for this excitement, as if in reality we should have created our own conflict. We should have done it with a different, but no lesser, fear, with the same trickle of sweat running down our backbone, just like those who provoke real danger, as if we too were gambling with our last and our beyond-our-last instants, from instant to instant. Still we do not know whether we are perceiving these events as spectators or if he, the matador, needs to sense the myriad gazes upon him. We could also mention the heat of these gazes and then describe them as lashes of a whip. Because of this, because of the arrows of these gazes raining down (which are still neither anxious energies nor life-saving ropes offering safety, and not even as reins and bits which contain or restrain detours into danger), can he embed himself into the other in such a way that, although he exists for the trinity, he experiences no more than duality. The third dissolves into the two, but meanwhile precisely this appreciation of duality brings him final eternal solitude. In this trinity, the one who pays attention, and the other, the one who is paid attention to, constantly exchange places, and because this torrent becomes a vision and the vision becomes a torrent, the witness becomes a conqueror and the conqueror becomes a murderer. The murderer becomes a sacrifice and the sacrifice again becomes a murder. The one who instigates the murder, because this stage show, this most ancient archetype and the real content of all stage shows, again and again lives out the sentence a man related to love once pronounced, a man who carries his own duality within himself and carries the duality of the created world, and who unknowingly in his own person plays the third between my thought and myself. The essence and knowledge he gleaned from this mysterious stage show is that this should exist, so that we may live out this real duality – as long as we recognize an equality between vision and reality.

What is the source of the spring of our courage that teaches us to perceive our thought in the mirror of the lake and in the duality of the border between the surface of the water and the air? We discover this fine hairline crack on the border between the two moving worlds of air and water, in the medium of our existence, and the imperceptible contour line between appearance and reality is darker and sharper than the colour of the entire body. How dare we, intoxicated, assess by a draught of clear water or a current in the clear air and regard as baseless what we have previously accepted as the basis of our existence? Because until we became spectators at this blood-boltered stage show *of the other*, we always believed that reality was simply what we saw and what we saw we always believed to be real. And what we accept as reality we believed to be constantly visible, even if only as possibility; that this possibility might become real we were never in any doubt. Now half the space within our knowledge is filled with darkness, just as the stone bulk of the arena denies half the sunlight of this summer afternoon, its shadow drawing sharp lines between light and dark, so sharp that we cannot question this other reality, what light has now become for us. Within our eyes this line is simply the distinct manifestation of light itself. We perceive the actuality, the substance, of two different worlds. And, in truth, it does not demarcate matter containing different energies. Are we not ourselves another body and another soul in the sun's brilliance, which, in our imagination, is the equivalent of the fine substance of freedom, which does not permit us to move in all directions, but with its soft and silky medium is equivalent to the airy and weightless illusion of so doing? We are not different in the black velvet density of the night, which adheres to us, makes our outlines vanish, squeezing us together evenly from all sides between the layers of this heavy porous carbon dust, so that we ourselves become unutterably dense. We become our own essence, as the contours turn inwards, drawing the boundary lines only from within, and the inner world becomes invisible because our essence, whatever we perceive, is not what we are ourselves. We ourselves are incapable, with our own eyes and our own senses, of achieving a knowledge of our own visibility. And thus we need to recognize our visible consciousness in the medium that emanates solely from the invisible. This is why we need this game, in which the visible half of our duality resurrects the invisible half of the symbolizing darkness before us. There is one who assists and protects and there is the eliminator, who at the end of the game will suffer his own elimination and be the agent of our elimination. The movement of these two other beings is fixed immutably into ourselves. The higher and the lower, human knowledge and animal awareness here compete with each other. The one who plays for us – and for himself as well – his every movement is rooted in the seed of visibility and flashes in the sphere of the visible. Its source is deeper than this, akin to the one who cannot distinguish the visible from the invisible, in whom beauty assumes form, not embodied within the world but that which we named as the principle of two and the principle of three, but in the medium of an unknowing being, who, without perceiving himself, can perceive the opposite half in a different way, with no concept of his own being within the conflict. The dance of the matador is his own life threatened: a balancing on the tightrope drawn between darkness and light. And what for us as spectators is a stimulating entertainment, for the bull is a struggle untranslatable into our language. And as spectators we perceive the duality; we see sympathy in the human and the sacrificial role of the animal, and in the intensity of this sunlit afternoon we perceive too how two forces metamorphose into each other, again and again submerging the one into the other. We see the matador in the intensity of the conflict become the bull, whose destiny we recognize . . . Yet we do not regret this; we fear it, even within ourselves we fear it. We do not know what inspires the greater excitement: in this fateful game do we identify with the matador, do we journey some distance with him, arousing and maddening the *Ur*-beast, the living symbol even now of some long-dead immortal god? As we watch the conflict, we scarcely realize that lying deeper than every one of our thoughts is a soul simultaneously identifying with the worshipped god, whom we fear because he springs from our own strength, from our own darkness. We do not know whether this bull was created out of the presence of this ancient god living within us, becoming within us the vision in the reality of the arena and the animal forced to run round the wooden wall becomes identical with ourselves. And thus we cannot tell the greater fear: murderous rage or inevitable destruction.

The trinity which always manifests itself in the image of duality appears only in the reality the third senses as a vision. The dance of this trinity slithers on the threshold where the one is extracted from the other two. If we envisage this trinity as the tangle of intertwined vines, it is ripped to shreds by the rage of the perpetually running bull. From instant to instant the duality shifts: sometimes I perceive the matador and the bull sinking the one into the other, so that they may not take cognizance of me. Their world is no longer the world of duality but has narrowed to a singularity, floating beyond physical existence, where the body despairs of maintaining its own intrinsic existence. In his every instant, here in his last lived instant, even then taking that gamble, hovering between existence and nothingness, which is like standing on the very last edge of life, on the glistening sand, building and destroying, again and again, the tumbling artefact. Out of the vision of nothingness and the immutability of nothingness the dance is a phenomenon of metamorphosis both lesser and greater than any art. All the greatest works of art take the route of enforced guarding or enforced submission. All are born of the conflict with nothingness, and what inspires more despair and hopelessness than the result of the conflict, as the arena presses ever tighter, as those who fight with each other are almost compressed into singularity? Or we can perceive the same thing as making space more and more limitless at the point where they are compressed together, so limitless and boundaryless that we no longer feel the density of the air heavy with moisture and sweat exuded by the compressed bodies. We experience it as unbearably thin, as if the atoms of oxygen have become ungraspable, rushing into the unreachable distances away from each other; we sense ourselves drowning in this vast expanse. As the bullring becomes tighter or wider, the blade becomes sharper and the embers glow more brightly and there is a greater tension in the artefact. The weapon adopts the movement of the wielder's hand, adapts to it. We exist within it only after the outcome of the battle, as resonant ancient memory, pupils narrowed to the size of a needle's point, with rivulets of sweat dampening our matted hair, like a veil of tears, clouding our vision. The blows exist as if in the past, blows that shake the body to its base that set up a continuing quivering that the ankles cannot steady. Because this conflict is in letters, images, musical notes, print, it can never vanish. It is not a stone falling into the water which with its ever widening and caressing rings soothes and smoothes the mirror of the lake, and it is not sound, where sound as its waves dwindle to nothing becomes silence. The sound remains in the chilled air, in this frozen motionless medium in which the transmission of sound waves has become impossible but in which there is always the possibility of eternally rippling rings. In reality, once this play of rings can revive, then the rippling can again begin the tinkling of the glass bells. The soul frozen in the moment of life endangerment melts again and again. From the half area of darkness the sunshine bursts through. Every instant that it turns to face the third, here and now with the spectator, it gathers fresh strength into itself. We spectators, sitting in the other half of the arena, do not realize that we are hearing the current of fear ringing and clanging ever more wildly, or, on the contrary, the challenge of danger in the flourishing of cloth. All we see is a dance unfolding before us, opening and closing like the steps of every dance, which, in its mysterious depth, is deeper than the movement of tumbling into the deep, which distinguishes and differentiates the dance from its steps. And it dignifies art, which emanates from the crushing death of the bullfight, which was born of the freedom of death.

Sometimes the matador is aware of the bull and the spectators. He sees them well even when his eyes are so riveted on his opponent that the gaze of the spectators is not now distinguishable from the gaze deepening into himself. Attention and terror (if we have managed to step beyond terror) both have one single frightening concentrated instant in which all that is outside disappears and all that was outside sinks within us in a rippling motion or an arabesque. Here everything compresses into one single action, an absolute action, so minute that it is not even perceptible as a movement. In truth there exists within time a glittering fissure, the instant when the arrow holds still in the air, and this movement precedes another, when the arrow penetrates the heart finally and for ever. In the instant before death, when the torn film whirls into endlessness, in this chillingly frozen image we glimpse the approaching horns of the bull, as if somewhere beneath us, suddenly stopping in mid-air in the region of the abdomen. Only the wind draws near, the air spun by the tips of the horns ever denser between body and body. It is the wind that this netherworld creature pushes before itself, dark and noxious, a choking underground air, racing towards the underworld of the knight's abdomen. It draws near in order to dissolve into pain the scintillating stars of the radiance of existence, the myriad shining stars, the extraordinary richness of maleness and within this richness the promise of endless rapture. But now it is only the rushing itself that flows, and the standing radiates black bushels of light, rays, dappling and glittering in the alternating surges of sunlight and shadow. Here stands the one at whom the lances point; these invisible mystical weapons draw near and pause on the hairline between fear and safety. He balances, swinging on a rope, and for one single instant he is aware of himself, the focal point of the horrified and awestruck gazes of the spectators. He sees himself, as if through a mist, in a blurring blood-red light, which seals him into itself. In the instant before penetration he is already experiencing unbearable pain, he senses it before it happens, within those fragments of glittering time which are themselves the very essence of whole entertainment and the art. This instant is the obverse of those other untold instants, before the danger, but after the danger, when the danger has already passed and in the next instant time stops in a decelerated movement of cloth after the *torrero* lunges forward. As for us, we who sit in a circle in the grandstand on striped concrete benches, we sense these instants turn the opposite way inside us and we perceive danger outgrowing destiny, this final turning away not as an existable existence, a turning away that is infinitely slow, the sliding of feet in the dust, the touch of a cat's paw on the ground, a movement in which we can perceive only alertness and the sidestep of an agile wild animal. We see the man as more agile and exercising greater craft than his opponent, but he himself is also a wild beast, and in this tense fight to the finish becomes so. Truly a wild beast? In his soul a man is able to identify with his opponent and in the battle for his own life he perceives an image or an echo of the battle of the other fighting for his life. In this mirror play, at once and always the duality, himself and his opponent, man and animal, each radiantly metamorphoses into the other. As animal, he is sluggish, bulky, terrifyingly strong, the destructive Minotaur, and yet he is also the agile, lizard-limbed, concealing, deceiving, dancing, imitative man–woman. In his strength and power a man and in his enticing attractiveness a woman; in his body a man and in his soul a woman, and he is able to follow to the very end the wanderings of this life-and-death tightrope dance, because in body and soul he is indivisible, inseparable as the sun and the moon. As the day and the night persecute each other, he escapes the death offered by the other, or the penetration dissolving his masculinity, more horrifying than death, and he opens himself to the agony of submerging himself into the other.

Is there some interdependence between the running of the bulls round the arena and the tumbling of the stars on a spring night, when the flowing rivers of the earth are simply a mirror image of the heavens? The cantering of the celestial herds can only echo the fragments of grief that hasten here from barren, crimson, stony hillsides and cottages nestling in the earth. It is the echo of passionate, fiery sobbing, the turning of a key in the lock, a pressure on the door handle and quiet discreet steps; the pain of the final leave-taking in the tangled sheets beneath the crumpled counterpane which unknown hands have sculpted to preserve the imprint of intertwined bodies. The moisture has no smell; no aroma lingers here for ever and evaporates for ever with the passing of the night, with the night that blazed with ecstasy, whose flame falls into ashes and whose star is extinguished. There is no God capable of caressing away the creases from the white coverlet of the soul, of drying the tears that never leave the corner of the eye, of wrenching the young girl away from the white doorpost, which she clings to as tightly as earlier she clung to that other body; this clinging is stronger than anything else, because she is clinging to a mast, fastened firmly in the pounding of the waves, waves reaching up to the sky, not taking into itself the thunder of the sea, a curved pole that straightens with the earthquake's shudder or perhaps a branch from the tree of the cross which nailed him to his agony.

In this turned world, where the silver of the moon bleaches the night into whiteness, it is not the white flock of the stars but the black bull of the earth that abducts the abandoned bride, Earth, to be one among the stars and our only star, the matter of which we are made and to which we shall return, after the great adventure, the adventure of abduction. We are abducted for ever, for he disappeared from our life, he who fights with the bull who abducts us, the man disguised as Minotaur, stealing our heart again and again, as we disappear into it, searching for and seeking out a refuge from the labyrinth. In truth we can never again escape from the zigzags and nooks and crannies of this labyrinth, its rounded arches and its twisted corners, its hidden dawn and its opaquely dark blind alleys. We wander in the blind alleys of our own soul, along the boundary between the inner world and the outer world, which means rather than boundary between that which is destined and that which is not destined. We ordered the creation of this maze ourselves, wanting to assume that chilling fear, the rumble of hoofs in the distance, now nearer, a thunderous drumming, the terror of being torn to shreds. This is fear we demand from the unconscious we ourselves wove, like the bewitched Ariadne, out of the spider thread of our terror and our longing. We descend into this captivity night after night, the desire to confine ourselves arising from the desire to become a pure and absolute sacrifice and from the fear that the smoke from the sacrifice of ourselves does not ascend towards the sky.

This is a blind and humiliating suffering, slithering along the smooth walls, in the maze of our existence and our non-existence. But yet more awful is that instant when, still not reaching the chamber, against every hopelessness, at least we attain the dawn, not trusting in the accuracy of our own vision, glancing at the sun, the gate, the exit, which once we have stepped through will become for us an entrance, the myrtle bushes and the rocky hillside. But if we look away for a single instant, our eyes cannot find their way back and we sob in the agony of liberation, not now from the blazing of love but because we sense ourselves as disinherited from the mesh of the fate that was woven for us. That is the reason that again and again we seek our heroes from the stars in their human embodiments, the bull eternally turning on itself and in its final jeopardy spilling its water and wine, and the matador, who exists as if with the existence of the bull, and the fight itself, which cannot rest between the two of them. The fight is emblematic of the struggle between us and the world, between the world and love, and between love and death, flicking its *muletas* in our souls. Not once, not twice, in the course of our life it severs our main arteries, allowing the black blood to spurt inside us and to flow as a river. For this reason we seek again and again the blood-boltered fight, as an image of the struggle flooding our own souls, which is for higher stakes than life or death. Again and again we die within the question of our death, which we ourselves awaken: is our destiny random or is our fate embedded in this instant in the bullfight in the starry sky?

And art, the companion, hovers around the game, sometimes identifying with it, plunging deep inside and then breaking outwards, like the tree's crown of foliage, its new branches twisting out of the old bark. It is like crystal, the essence of crystal, emerging from the oversaturated solution of the world, the creation, almost diffusing the ice cold of nonexistence. From the heart of action emanates its inner stasis, from life matter that is in essence lifeless, or which renders of the possibility of life incomprehensible. Away from our sensations, from our love, from our faith, from our devotion, our fear diffuses that which is alien to our life, the rippling movement halted: death is held fast in our existence. Like this blood-boltered game, which is more ancient than the drama of man in conflict with man, this tired drama of man in conflict with man, performed for others, reverts to a more solitary and more symbolic scene, where the soul of man is set against the underworld and the soul of dance reveals itself.

Our fate breaks away from our soul, by the light of our own stars, and out of our fate, the pattern of the carpet of the soul, a winding pattern emerges, which leads one, finally, into the meanderings of the labyrinth, a destiny more glorious than our own. The map, like the crooked geometries of a power raised to infinity, cannot be represented with the drawings and wanderings of this world. This takes place in the medium of the indefinable, on the boundary between our fate and our consciousness. This consciousness does not dwell in the empire of things inexpressible in language; neither does it dwell in the dawning gloom of uncertainty but in the spaceless fissure of existence. It will be made plain, with us, with what happens with us and what happens within us, in the gathering together and in the sundering of our secret existence and our otherwise secret earthly life. The winding flow of thought meanders and if we abandon understanding, it will be the only road, the only way to transform the incomprehensible into an object of devotion: a symbol. The symbol becomes once more that which we once perceived in the depths of our existence, in the struggle before still human self-knowledge, in the merciless sadism of man towards bull in earlier days – and not just in the arousing of the animal to the point of unconscionable rage in which it charges into its own death. With this fashion of killing, it is not only the gate to the bullring that opens, but the gate to the human soul, through which bursts, without restraint, the instinct of mercilessness. Not only mercilessness for the other, born for death and reared for murder, but a teasing, a tantalizing, the indirectness of the steps of the dance through which, again and again, we instigate murder. Is this mercilessness a greater sin, committed against the world, than a laying waste to ourselves, in a bitter confusion of the order of things? Is there a higher aspiration than our own selfhood, an irrational sacrificial gesture, in the game in which, without hope of redemption, we scratch our signs on the onyx black of the water mirror? Take delight in this mirror game for no other reason than the mystery of giving delight and being delighted.

What does that word mean; what is the meaning of the phenomenon of delight? Is it not simply a sudden coming into awareness, and the dance with its steps going first here and then there immediately bewitches with the regularity of seemingly random motion? Is it not the emergence of order from seeming chaos, a sudden glimpse of a hidden organization, laws that in truth we shall never come to know? The consequence of these pale guesses is to allow us to sense the world as permeated by the soul of God, filled with the invisible breath of creation. Is it not simply the meaning of beauty that we should see the world and God himself bound by a magic circle of a greater power? We perceive beauty as if it is the place of origin, from where the soul originates, the power of the waters of God, the sign of gold and silver. We perceive it as the reflected light of such a reality, which it is not given to us to absorb but only to guess at. Perhaps beauty's suggestion is our life's certainty. We can come to know God and we can come to know the soul of the world only in the light of this suggestion, enchanted and humbled. And does not beauty itself spring out of our existence, staggering without governance between a random sequence of events and a path of pre-ordained destiny? In a narrow fissure, in the metamorphosis of chaos and rhythm the one into the other. Whence comes the revolving wind, which, now here, now there, drives us to first one bank and then the other bank of the river, which mirrors for us two different worlds, the linear game of the sand dunes of time and the crystal palaces of eternity? And whence comes the suffering, which, an echo of the revolving wind, picks us up and tosses us on to the other bank when we would have made our home in one of its territories? Here, in the intimacy of the transitory, among the rustling silk hangings and the glimmering yearning candle flames, in the warmth of a pair of hands enclosing our face between their palms, before his eyes let us fall from the silken web of his gaze. We fall but, as in an atmosphere of oxygen, for one instant our life gleams before us, glistens, but disappears in the inner warmth of the outer cold, in this momentary shower of sparks, this unlikely rain of light and colour, in which a glance is glistening gold. This unlikely rain of light and colour, this sensuality both clearer and more blurred than anything previously known, this sensuality bruises our skin. We disappear into the vision of the other, like an endless sequence of cathedrals unfolding each from the other, like a building that was expressly created only to allow us to awaken God's being within, with nothing but the magic numbers of a perfect measurable ratio. But the proportions of these cathedrals carry within themselves numbers larger than all else, slipping through the fissure of *as if*, into the incalculable; at such times it seems that precisely this is the essence of existence.

It is the essence of beauty, flashing between structure and the dawning of light, between life and fate, on the boundary of immersion and recognition, on a boundary that does not exist, because beauty does not mean just this, that we simply imagine the boundary and that beyond each drawing there vibrates another, created of its own oscillations, from its actuality and the mesh that wraps itself in its own radiation, and that looser mesh, though denser still, which only we see around it, the golden tangle of our memories, our feelings, our love. Is it not beauty that reminds us of the uncertainty of our existence, which we name as the uncertainty of actuality, and therefore, that beauty in our eyes implies the createdness of the world; is it not precisely this that plants in our hearts our sense of him, he who perceived our world as certain and regular, lying in parallel? It is indefinable, irregular; numbers cannot press on into endlessness, because it was he who created number with unwritable letters, because the writing that he created from letters is none other than the illegible papyrus, the indecipherable oracle, of existence, which is not confinable between the boundaries of beginning and ending. It is the same as our failure to perceive the beginning and the ending of the game, nor, as if we could foresee it, the curves drawn as it were with a silver pencil in the air, showing vines running into one another and breaking away from one another, in movement, fragments of life. This opaquely regular geometry is recorded on the earth in the incalculable movements of mathematics, with its unconscious imitations, illuminating the curves of geometry and the invisible gravitational forcefields of the stars, though we may not perceive them, in the obscurity of the borderlands between life and fate.

It is this that, since we have been able to recognize it, we call beauty. Did we not step with this recognition into the uncertain medium of human existence? Did we not shoulder this immeasurably heavy burden with this understanding? Fear, not of death but of the recognition that our destiny confines us between two infinities. Why should it be less significant that we think anxiously about where we came from rather than where we are going to? In the question is contained not simply the where but also the why. And these two questions serve only to conceal a much more profound, more deranged pain, that this precluded, fenced-in life is like that secretly chalked or waxed paper of our childhood which, when drawn or written on, say the story of some bygone event, would produce a pattern, a curlicue of winding lines of destiny. And does not what we name beauty build up this same meandering pattern from the invisible imprint of our existence? From existence, which is not the same as fate, we derive the important and the personal, for the braids of life and fate, now shining, now pulling the drawn pattern of our life into identity, in the same way and in this same intangible medium twines together our own destiny with one more powerful than our own. It is as if our soul were a lake on an island taking its water from the sea, surging with a regular rhythm, yet this water is fresh water, filtered through the bitterness and sweetness of our destiny, through the pebbles, the clay, the top soil, the humus, in which, from the deconstructed cells of the human dead, new plants cell form, still guarding within themselves the bitter aroma of salt, the heaving and endless bitterness overshadowing from birth to death the light cast across our single life illuminated as it is by flashes of lightning. Beauty triggers the bud of invisibility to bloom, which renders itself visible with the contours of shadow and terror and which moulds the indeterminacy of our existence, with lines, with sound, with movement, with words, into something determined, into such a visible, audible, tangible and conceivable reality, which in actuality is simply an image, an echo, a vibration in the air and a metaphor for reality, but which itself is more abstract and higher than itself, its essence raised on to another plane, glittering down on itself and the light of this reflected glow will seem in our eyes a reality. This reflection makes real for us once more that which in our eyes had once seen as the roots of these forms, which are now above reality.

In this following from each other, which seemingly is a following on from each other, in that movement in time, in which the two instants are superimposed, the vibration of their touching seems to produce the susurrus of the bird wings of transitoriness. The decaying of flowers conjures beauty from the truly transitory; it cannot co-exist with the transitory and therefore cannot exist within time. Music wove from this transitoriness a dense copper mesh, a tissue of hair-fine golden wire not identifying itself with transitoriness, a form of life already beyond passing existence and past existence, not within timelessness but within time compressed into itself. It is as if – but only as if – that which was once not perceived as seeable leaps into the field of being. It projects itself into forms that are real only for us, springing into shape from within us so that the truth of this createdness becomes visible in the world that we ourselves created. Our nets lifted these forms up out of the world and inside us the created world was created from itself, and just like the world, the creator of all things created us too. These forms are parts of the substance of the world just as much as we are ourselves. Not simply parts or fragments of the originating substance, but denser than that, more concentrated, matter obedient to other laws, that which existed in the filtered essence of the substance of our souls. But if not from elsewhere, as from the border of the suspected known and the feared unknown world, and what trembling they stir, the butterfly-wing shadows of beauty conjure the world into our home. And with nothing other than the unavoidable notion of createdness. Because of this we should be grateful to beauty that we are able to bear the weight of our arrival and departure. And we can be grateful to beauty that sometimes our vanishing succeeds in taming terror into the dance steps of time. Instead of giving way, rather summoning and challenging, because beauty does not conceal but highlights, makes what is intolerable tolerable, and with the compulsion to tolerate, it presents for us the unbearableness of that death, before which we cannot close our eyes. It gives our human existence understanding and essence and every single blow of beauty is the ringing of a bell audible from a great distance.If we dare to submerge our entire heart to make contact with beauty, with our naked soul, like lovers greeting, then we shall drink from the dark spring water of death, until it intoxicates our life.

Are we not born for this drunkenness, for the vertigo of dread, fear and pain, the anaesthetizing dizziness without which we could not reach the end of our road? We arrive nowhere, yet continually we move forwards. We move forward without the distance between us and the end of our road ever lessening, because this road has no end, and perhaps no beginning either, because we cannot remember a beginning and we cannot imagine an end. So how may we conceive distance, the length of a step, the length of the road on the island, on the banks of the lagoon? Whence comes our notion of the mystery of the golden section, the spell of disintegration, and this merciless and mild-mannered magician of time? From him who makes the wall between the green moss and the black mirror of the water glow purple, which we recognize as the setting of the sun, that the sun does not revolve but sets? Whence comes our knowledge that it sinks into the sea and that tomorrow, when we shall no longer see it, that it will rise again?

How can we remember, again and again, those who no longer watch the lights, or who perhaps watch and cannot see them? Whence came our image of the blindness of the dead? Perhaps they see otherwise, within the immeasurable richness of a single instant, and therefore, in the tangling together of forms they perceive different structures, which are still unbearable in our glimmering life. Whence comes our notion of the dead but from death itself, which presents itself as the rupturing of life, as its continuation or as its mirror image, although the transformation, in the instant of our stepping across the threshold, perhaps lifts our existence on to a higher and richer plane of being. Perhaps what we perceive here as curtailing and elimination is perceived there as completion.

Because we always swallow the water of life and the water of death together, the drizzle of fear and dread soaks the fabric of our life through and through, fills it with light and colour; otherwise we would not feel its ever-present threat; we would see as beautiful distinctions in the over-rich material, the sparkling of light on the waves of the sea, the different layers sliding into one another and overshadowing one another, the rays of light continually reflecting and changing colour, shaping the forms of the world. Because we do not know, we see – like a compressed seed of our life, like the source of our devotion springing up, like the candle flame guttering before it blows out, shining more golden in the velvet darkness than any cooling gold, like hills drawn with a silver wand, twisting valleys and waterfalls, like land folded in on itself – the border country between life and death, a passageway beneath the earth with its currents of air and its veins of water. We do not know whether created matter conceals these forms within itself, that it guards them throughout endless time, hiding its createdness continually deeper and deeper in its concealed well, until an eye peeping over it just glimpses it, out of the gloaming more sharply etched on the marble-black mirror. Or is it the eye that gives form to the shape because ancient forms hide inside it, and it is able to project them on to the surface of the world?

The beginning and the end, the gate that gives definition to all things, the quadrille gate, opposite the other one, through which the bull enters the arena and even the boards lining the entrance and the concrete, encircle everything capable of being seen by us. These two gates are not intentionally placed to face each other symmetrically across the arena. This continuously symmetrical-seeming world does not float on an axis; it is not balanced like the arms of a pair of scales. If the axis is our existence, and our birth and death two rods laid at right-angles, from their continuous trembling we must sense that our birth and our death are not the two end-points of our life fitting into each other, just as beauty cannot be crushed either by the world hidden within itself, or by the transparent forms we perceive within it.

What raises the bullfight above simple conflict and a simple game of destruction and what makes it float between the rhythm of unconscious steps and the dance of the red of the *muleta* is the completed existence of the present. It mirrors the water of our soul in that what happens on the surface of the arena, and only on the surface of the arena, is also the mirror image of the game below the surface in the water of our soul. The bullfight is not only the desire for and the fear of danger, and not just the knowledge of it (in which the matador learns to respect the skill of the bull, without realizing that he is invoking the strength of a greater power). It is not simply the courage springing from the strength of the opponent being in reality unimaginable, but it creates itself out of the presence of exultant beauty and exultant despair pouring the one into the other and disappearing the one into the other, turning existence into non-existence. The hand of the clock slowly crosses the black numeral, towards the instant of the blinding burst of light and the showering sparks of its unbearable blind darkness.

I did not finish this book. I put it to one side. More than eighteen months passed before I decided to publish it. I stopped working on it briefly, while some other text took form within me and demanded to be expressed – that is what I thought at the time. But then I was unable to continue with it. What had died – or dried up – inside me? I had hazarded at the possibility of *between*, and the tense arc of writing between the past and the future broke, the words tumbled off their thread, and darkness swallowed them up. Did those words become seeds in the soil? It is not impossible that they will grow into something. But what? I don't know the answer to that.

Please, if you read this book through to the end, try, without the words existing there in front of you, to listen for the final, unwritten chapter: *Between Silence and Muteness.*